CRAFT BUSINESS POWER

*15 Days To A Profitable
Online Craft Business*

By Jason G. Miles & Cinnamon Miles

Free Gift

Dear *Craft Business Power* Readers,

As a thank you for picking up a copy of the book I'd like to give you another ebook - free...

I thought I'd share this resource with you in the off chance you are trying to understand how to make money with Instagram. My new marketing efforts are focused on Instagram monetization strategies and I've just finished a new book coming out with McGraw Hill. It documents our lessons learned. As part of the project I made a free ebook focused on Visual Product Launches on Instagram. If you'd like a free copy just go to http://www.instagrampower.com.

Also by Jason G. Miles

Pinterest Power

Instagram Power

Price It Like Picasso

Email Marketing Power

Liberty Jane Media
CRAFT BUSINESS POWER
15 Days To A Profitable Online Craft Business
By Jason G. Miles & Cinnamon Miles

Published in the United States by Liberty Jane Media

Liberty Jane Media
P.O. Box 8052
Bonney Lake, WA 98391

ISBN-13: 978-1484065662

Printed by CreateSpace, a DBA of On-Demand
Publishing, LLC

About The Authors

Jason G. Miles is the co-founder of Liberty Jane Clothing and manages the marketing, writing, branding, and social strategy. Jason is also the co-author of *Pinterest Power*, an Amazon bestselling book. Jason's day job is serving as the Vice President of Advancement (marketing, development, and human resources) at Northwest University in the Seattle area. He also teaches at the university's School of Business Management. He holds a graduate degree in Business Administration, as well as undergraduate degrees in both Organizational Management and Biblical Studies.

Cinnamon Miles is the co-founder and lead designer at Liberty Jane Clothing, a rapidly growing craft business. Her design team includes a group of incredibly talented master designers and artisans focused on producing the world's best doll clothing. Cinnamon also serves as an official brand ambassador for Bernina, the world's premiere sewing machine company.

About Liberty Jane Clothing

Launched in 2008 with an emphasis on making custom patterned outfits for dolls, Liberty Jane is known for using top quality fabrics, creating trendy designs, and giving customers the chance to own something rare and beautiful. The company is also known for holding auctions that surpass 'normal' and escalate to ultra-premium prices.

Liberty Jane Clothing started as an eBay store, achieving PowerSeller status within only a few months. Today, Liberty Jane is a fast growing six-figure small business focused on delivering exceptional designs for the doll market as well as educational programs and tools for sewing enthusiasts and craft business owners.

In 2009, the company began selling patterns as PDF files. With over 250,000 patterns downloaded from LibertyJanePatterns.com, the site has become the #1 online source for doll clothes patterns. Working with over 20 independent designers, the site frequently publishes new patterns in support of many doll types and design traditions.

In 2010, the company started the Liberty Jane Partners program. By creating and publishing resources like this e-book, Liberty Jane encourages and assists sew-from-home entrepreneurs in using the patterns as the basis for their businesses. Now more than 1,200 partners work with Liberty Jane Clothing, taking advantage of this opportunity to earn additional income. Learn more about the Liberty Jane Partners program at LibertyJanePartners.com.

You can learn more about Liberty Jane Clothing at the following online locations:

www.libertyjaneclothing.com

www.libertyjanepatterns.com

www.libertyjanepartners.com

http://stores.ebay.com/libertyjaneclothing

http://www.youtube.com/libertyjaneclothing

https://www.facebook.com/LibertyJaneClothing

http://pinterest.com/cinnamonmiles/

http://instagram.com/libertyjaneclothing

Table of Contents

Introduction
By Cinnamon Miles

I first learned about American Girl dolls from a friend and her daughter. They had dolls, clothes, furniture, and magazines. So when my older daughter turned nine, I decided to buy her a doll. She really wanted two things: an American Girl doll and an outfit from Limited Too. To make the gifts even more meaningful, I had the idea of making a matching doll outfit for her new doll. Having our daughter Makena match her new doll seemed like a cute idea, so I went to the local fabric store and picked up a Simplicity pattern that seemed to be relatively similar.

The outfit turned out great after I changed a few things around. The process for making doll clothes was fairly easy for me because growing up my mom worked for a fashion house in Santa Monica, and she taught me to sew through making clothes for my 17-inch Kimberly doll. I used to make tons of clothes for Kimberly. My grandmother had a friend who worked in the cutting room at fashion designer Bob Mackie's studio, and I'll never forget the time she gave me a huge bag of fabric from his shop.

When my daughters got interested in American Girl, it felt really familiar to me, even though I hadn't been focused on doll clothes for more than 20 years. At first, I wasn't passionate about the doll clothes, however I was passionate about my daughters having great birthday parties and learning to sew.

Next came my other daughter Liberty's doll and a pile of matching dance outfits. When Liberty took them to the dance studio where she was taking lessons, I immediately had moms asking if they could buy outfits for their daughters' dolls. I asked the studio owner if I could buy some of the extra dance outfits so I could cut them up. This led me to the realization that there was a market for these types of custom American Girl clothes. You can see pictures of those original projects on the Liberty Jane Clothing Facebook fan page.

In January of 2008, my husband Jason asked if he could try to list one of the outfits on eBay. Together we decided to try to take this idea to a new level. Hannah Montana was all the rage at the time, and I decided to make an outfit that was similar to one on the front of her album. The idea of making contemporary clothes for these dolls became my passion. When I say contemporary, I mean scaled-down versions of current tween fashions. The designers call this being 'on trend.' That was the original concept that inspired the creation of Liberty Jane Clothing.

The nice part about this approach was that my

girls got to participate. They would cut out examples from catalogs and make homemade look books that said, 'Mom, make these' on the cover. I was the most popular designer for the third grade class at Tremont Elementary. That first year I was sewing as much as I could to meet demand.

In addition to having a mom who taught me to sew at a fairly high level, I also had a husband who was an info product junkie and was always buying books about marketing. He always wanted to build an online business. He saw what I was doing and instantly realized we had a product that could sell. After the hours of shopping for fabric, customizing designs, sewing, finishing outfits, and taking photos, I thought the work was done. All that was left was to sell the outfits.

Jason said, "Wait, you need a brand, a unique name for the outfit, a story, and you need to start the bidding at 99 cents. There is a ton of work left to do." When he said 99 cents I had a knot in my stomach. That was really hard for me to accept and we spent a long time talking about it. So we tried it one time to see if he was right, and that outfit sold for $39. That auction, ending higher than an authentic American Girl outfit, made us realize that there was a market for these clothes at a higher price point. Liberty Jane Clothing wouldn't be what it is today without all of these business decisions having been made well.

If you're like me, these are not the topics you like

to focus on or know how to approach. The goal of this book is to have all of these business concepts laid out in a simple-to-follow 15-day format. Our hope is that you can take your amazing and unique crafts and build a successful business in your niche.

Because these chapters deal with the business issues involved in a craft business, Jason is going to be the primary writer. To make sure you hear my perspective on each topic, we've included a Q&A section with each chapter, too. I hope you enjoy that part of it.

Finally, let me share a brief note about how to use this book. There are 15 chapters; each chapter has an action step, which is included at the end of the chapter. The lessons start simply, with very basic ideas. Don't worry—just commit to the process, complete the steps, and by the end of the 15 days, you'll be off to a great start. Businesses don't happen overnight, so we aren't suggesting that after 15 days you'll be done with the hard work; it will just be getting started.

You can do this!

Cinnamon Miles
Seattle, WA

Day #1

Catch a Fever

I'll never forget the night I heard about someone making $1,000 a day with an online business. It was 1998 and the Internet was still very new to all of us. Although I'm usually an early adopter, and had been using online services since 1995, I hadn't heard too many examples of people actually earning a living online. Email was the 'killer app' that most people were using at that point. Then there were message boards, new websites from various companies, and content on AOL, but there weren't that many obvious ways to make money online.

I was looking for a second job at the time, trying to make ends meet for my young family. Cinnamon and I had just had our first son, Jordan, so I was open to anything and everything that could help us get a little bit more income.

One Sunday evening, Cinnamon and I took Jordan to a home group meeting. I asked our group to pray for my job search, and someone said,

"Maybe you should connect with Steve — he's making $1,000 a day on the Internet and I think

he needs help."

Here is how the dialogue continued:

Me: *"$1,000 a day . . . on the Internet?"*

Them: *"Yeah, I guess his idea has really taken off."*

Me: *"That's $365,000 a year. Over the Internet?"*

Them: *"Yeah."*

Me: *"What does he do?"*

Them: *"He got a traffic ticket, then got frustrated that he had to actually go to an all-day traffic school to get it removed from his driving record. So he created an online traffic school training course and got the county judge to approve it as an acceptable online version of the regular program. The judge sends people to Steve's website, then they take the course and print out a certificate."*

Me: *"Wow, what's his number? I'm going to give him a call."*

"$1,000 a day on the Internet": those were the most magical words I had ever heard. It was like they went into my head and echoed for months — actually for years. In fact, they are still up there echoing loudly right now. I guess it's something similar to gold fever.

2

I did talk to Steve, and he needed someone for just a few hours a week. I needed more work than that, so I passed on the opportunity to work with him. That was probably a massive mistake, but life goes on. I've heard since then he's now making more like $4,000 per day.

Call us slow learners, but it took us 10 full years after that conversation happened to create our own online business. It was ten years of that phrase rattling around in my mind — "$1,000 a day online." Ten years of that idea haunting me every time I was stuck in traffic, every time I had a bad interaction with my boss, every time I felt like I was traveling too much for my job, every time we couldn't afford something and had to use a credit card. Why in the world did I wait 10 years? I have no good answer. But the idea never left the back of my mind, regardless of the highs or lows we were going through.

For several reasons, the time was finally right in 2008 and we launched Liberty Jane Clothing, an online business based on my wife's design talent. It started really small, with a $39 dollar sale on eBay, and it was a lot of hard work. The first financial goal was to start making $1,000 a month. My only regret is that we didn't start the business in 1998 when we first heard about Steve.

It was hard work. But isn't life hard work? Isn't working for other people hard work? Isn't the uncertainty of a career, and a mortgage, and a boss hard work? Isn't it hard work to keep your marriage solid when you are broke and you need to put gas in the car to get to work? Life is hard work. Why not channel it toward something that can ultimately set you free financially?

Five years later, and a full 15 years after catching the fever, I'm happy to report that we have a thriving six-figure business that is growing very quickly. Yesterday we had a sales total of $635. Today we brought in $1,405. We frequently make over $1,000 a day in total sales, although not every day. We believe that within a few years, Liberty Jane will be a million dollar business, which (if you're wondering) is $2,739 a day for 365 days in a row.

It is important to note that there is a big difference between total revenue and net revenue. Total revenue is how much you make in sales. Net revenue is how much you keep as profit after expenses.

Here is the short story of how we went from a $39 eBay sale to our current level of revenue. I won't go too deeply into each step, but this gives you the general idea.

Phase 1: From the beginning, Liberty Jane Clothing started making $1,000 each month via eBay auctions, and we did that for about 18 months. This required Cinnamon to sew for eight hours or more each day, which was clearly unsustainable. But it was a critical time when we established our brand, got a solid collection of fans, and started to learn about the doll clothes niche.

Phase 2: Then we launched Liberty Jane Patterns. This was a huge decision for us at the time, and one that we debated. The first month we sold 11 patterns. But it was a great next step, as it allowed us to sell digital items, which are a lot of work but have a very long 'shelf life.' We've gone on to create a publishing relationship with over 20 designers who all sell on our site.

Phase 3: We launched Liberty Jane Partners to help entrepreneurs with their sew-from-home businesses. At first, our patterns stated that 'you may not use this pattern for commercial purposes'—that was a big mistake. See, we thought we were going to prevent competition, but really that strategy would have simply provoked more competition. So instead we reversed our thinking 180 degrees, asking people to become our partners and use our patterns. As of the morning I'm writing this, we have 1,021 people who have agreed to be our partners. It costs them nothing, and we provide selling assistance. All we ask in return is that they include 'Made from a Liberty Jane Clothing Pattern' in their eBay or Etsy listing.

Phase 4: We launched a Premium Partners Program, which we've renamed 'The Cutting Room.' This is a paid membership club, where you can chat with Cinnamon and our other team members and get additional support. Members also get educational tips and tools as well as advertising support. The current price is $9.99 a month and we are adding new members each week. The beauty of this type of online effort is recurring billing, aka monthly subscription pricing. If you have 200 people giving you $9.99 a month, it adds up.

Phase 5: We launched an e-book entitled *The Design Academy.* Then we realized we could actually use that book as the basis of a one-month-long training program. We call it 'The Design Academy Course' and run it several times a year for $79. It is taught by Cinnamon and Karin Pascho, a member of our design team who worked as a Senior Designer at Nordstrom for many years.

Phase 6: In 2011, we started a new blog about marketing on Pinterest, MarketingOnPinterest.com. Our writing and publishing efforts jumped up to the 'professional' level when we published *Price It Like Picasso* on Amazon and got a publishing deal with McGraw Hill for a book about Pinterest. Our first 'real' book was *Pinterest Power*, which is currently an Amazon bestseller in the Small Business Marketing category and is also available in print everywhere books are sold. The success of that book led to another formal contract for two more books. Those will be in bookstores and on Amazon in 2013.

Future Phases: So how will we get to our new goal of $2,739 a day? In the future, we believe we can generate more revenue by publishing sewing books formally, which we're working to coordinate. We can also take our Liberty Jane brand into the tween girls' clothing space with hoodies and t-shirts. We can also increase the volume of the doll clothes we sell. Finally, we can continue to serve the craft business market with books similar to this one. We've also started to think about how to become a blessing to more people. We've set up a charity, SewPowerful.org, to help women in poor countries learn to sew and sell.

Have you caught the fever? I hope so.

Can I give you one simple trick that will start you on the path toward that exciting '$1K Per Day' goal? Here it is:

Taking a simple action step toward your goal is critical. Now that you have a goal, be like a dog with a bone. Bury it, dig it back up, gnaw on it, sleep with it, and bury it again. Do not lose that bone. It's yours if you want it, and no one can take it away. On Day #2, we'll talk about why taking those initial steps is so important.

As we finish up this chapter, let me share the single most important lesson of this book right up front, so you won't accuse me of being too vague about how to achieve your craft business success.

There is a concept in entrepreneurship documented by Robert Ronstadt, a professor at the University of Illinois, which he called the Corridor Principle. Have you heard of it? It states:

> *"Just by starting . . . entrepreneurs become aware of other startup opportunities they would not have seen nor taken advantage of if they had not [started]."*

In other words, once you start down a path toward a goal, doors of opportunity will begin to appear and open that would never have been visible to you if you hadn't started down the path in the first place. Starting down the path is the key part. You just need to start moving toward an entrepreneurial venture and the doors will magically start to appear. I'm not saying it will be easy, but if you start moving forward then you'll see exciting things happen.

Make the decision to follow this e-book's 15-day action step plan. Don't delay the launch of your product; don't procrastinate or make an excuse. Ninety-five percent of people who hear this idea will make an excuse for not starting. They'll tell you all the reasons that it's a bad time for them to start a business. But if you want to see success, then you've got to take that first step.

Just start. Magic will begin to happen. You will discover what countless entrepreneurs have found before you — that the willingness to jump in, even if you don't know what you're doing, is the single greatest factor in your success.

Author Joe Vitale has wisely said,

> *"It's easier to make dollars if you've made pennies first. It's easier to make hundreds after you've made a few dollars. It's easier to make thousands if you've made hundreds."*

Fix the goal in your mind clearly and don't let it go:

You are going to learn how to sell online.

I love this quote:

> *"Whatever you do, or dream you can, begin it. Boldness has genius and power and magic in it."*

> - frequently attributed to Johann Wolfgang von Goethe

Chapter One Q&A with Cinnamon:

Jason: Do you remember hearing about Steve and his $1,000-a-day Internet business?

Cinnamon: I don't remember it — I was probably changing a diaper — but I remember you wouldn't stop talking about it afterwards. I thought you was a little OCD about the whole thing.

Jason: But did you ever think you could make $1000 per day online?

A: No. But I remember that when we started to regularly make $100 a day, we started talking about it. We started to think that it was possible. I think you and I think very differently on this topic. My goals are more project-level goals. Things like — what are the pieces of the next collection, what pattern should we put out next, what am I going to make for dinner?

Jason: What motivated you to work so hard at the beginning? Why would you sew for eight hours a day?

Cinnamon: Well, it was easy to hit the 're-list' button on eBay and sell another copy of the exact same item, but then I had to sew it. The motivation from the beginning was that we needed money. It was easy to sell it on eBay, but not as easy to make it. So I knew as much as I could sew, I could sell. I was making a lot of items, listing them as 'buy-it-now' to make customers happy and provide them with items they wanted. I was listing separates like tops and pants that I had to sew. That was a mistake.

Jason: What's your next goal for the business?

Cinnamon: I don't think my goal would be financial. Some of my goals would be to be more organized and consistent with our pattern publishing, to begin to work farther ahead in terms of the Spring and Fall Lines, and to continue to learn how to grow the team.

Day #1 Action Step: Find a startup story that inspires you. Set up a journal that you'll use for the next 15 days as you prepare to launch or grow your craft business. Write about why you love the startup story you've found. Write down the aspects of the founder's journey that you want to try to emulate. Write down a clear goal related to starting your online business.

Day #2

How to Build a Castle

Warren Buffett, the best investor of all time, posts his annual shareholder letters online for anyone to view. They are packed with business ideas and great quotes — some inspirational and others humorous. This is one of his famous quotes:

> "In business, I look for economic castles protected by unbreachable moats. An 'economic castle' is a great business, and the 'unbreachable moat' is the strategy or market dynamic that heightens the barriers-to-entry and makes it difficult or ideally impossible to compete with, or gain access to, the economic castle."

In other words, he likes businesses that can't be easily damaged by competitors or things like changing customer preferences, inflation, shifting technology, or government policy changes. A financial fortress of a business — that's what the smartest investor in the world is looking for. He buys companies like See's Candies, Coca-Cola, and GEICO Insurance.

Don't we do the same thing when we think about choosing a career? We wonder which career will sustain our family fortunes for the long-term and will weather storms in the economy.

Can you create a financial castle, right from your home, in such a way that it cannot be easily damaged? Can a craft business provide the answer? You can obviously create a financial castle by becoming rich, but what about before you become rich?

Can you bulletproof your household income so that regardless of what happens, you're fine? Most people assume that this level of safety is only possible if you obtain that elusive 'rich' status, but that is simply not true. You can create safety, bulletproof your income, and make your household income into a castle with an unbreachable moat. You can do it by building an online business that provides consistent income.

To start to ensure that your finances are unbreachable, you can build a financial cushion — financial advisor Dave Ramsey calls this an emergency fund. It helps you overcome the financial trauma that seems to be a natural part of life.

We're all familiar with the financial onslaughts that weaken our castle walls:

- loss of your primary income
- rising costs of food and housing

- an unforeseen expense explosion
- destruction of your nest egg by stock market losses
- a chronic shortage of cash
- theft
- massive medical bills
- lack of retirement savings
- underwater mortgages due to the housing market collapse
- lack of economic opportunity in your city
- stiff competition, either for jobs or for customers

Any one of these would be bad enough to deal with, but sadly, they tend to pile up. There are times when frustrations quickly converge and threaten to ruin our happiness and our finances. They take turns, mix together, and create a very powerful chain of financially destructive events. The castle can feel like it is under attack.

You might wonder why we are so excited about helping people build a home-based business of their own. The answer is simple.

When we started our business in 2008, we were battling our own financial crisis. We really needed Liberty Jane Clothing to work. I won't bore you with all the sad details, but we had purchased a home in Northern California in 2005, right at the height of the housing bubble, and we had (stupidly) used a toxic mortgage. We saw our monthly mortgage increase to an insane amount and the value of our house drop. We simply couldn't afford to pay our monthly mortgage even though we were trying our best.

Ultimately we lost that house, but not before we started to build a small business that had the potential to change everything. Our first goal was $1,000 a month. While we realized we might not be able to salvage our mess, we knew that starting our own business could certainly be part of the long-term solution. Now we are passionate about helping people in similar circumstances. We regularly hear from our partners that they are desperate to make an extra $200 a month to make ends meet. That their spouse just got laid off. That they are battling significant medical costs and urgently need to earn more money. We can honestly say that we feel a very deep burden to help people in these situations.

Let me ask you, what would $100 a day in new income mean for your monthly finances? That is $36,000 a year.

In 2010, the median household income in the U.S. was $45,800. So an extra $100 a day, or $36,000 a year, would increase the average American's household income by a whopping 78%. To double the average household income of $45,800 through online sales, you only need to make an extra $125 a day.

According to a recent New York Times article, to be considered a member of the wealthiest 10% of American households, you need to earn $349,000 a year. To do that through online sales, you need to make $956 a day for the full year.

Of course, $100 a day or $1,000 a day are ideas that are about more than just the money. Making money online means making money from home, instead of via a long commute. It means making money in your pajamas instead of 'business casual' attire. It means earning money (and this one is huge) seven days a week instead of five days a week. It means earning money 24 hours a day instead of from 9 to 5. These advantages of online revenue versus a traditional job are incredibly important to understand.

But it's also more than any of that stuff. An online income means the freedom to say to any boss — "see ya." It means creating a source of income that you control completely and that is bulletproof, fireproof, recession-proof, and idiot-proof.

You've taken the initiative to get this book, load it up, and sit down and read it, so you're motivated to improve your finances and strengthen your home's economic fortunes. Right? That's a great first step: you are already on your way. Call this e-book your 'Base Camp.' It's the starting point on your journey to making $1,000 per day. Install '1K Per Day' in your brain like a new long-term life goal. Forget retirement. Shoot for '1K Per Day.' Maybe it will take you 15 years like it did us, but let me tell you from experience, it goes by faster than you might think.

So it is time to choose a short-term goal. Do you need $1,000 a month? More? I can't promise you any specific success by reading this book, but I can promise you this: you must take responsibility for your craft business success. You must make a financial goal and work toward it.

You must decide that rather than letting life destroy your finances, you're going to use those difficult situations to jumpstart your craft business and become a successful online seller. You're going to use concentration, speed, momentum, and surprise. You're going to turn your stress into motivation. You're going to get fired up and admit that you are in a war, that the enemy is real, and that the stakes are incredibly high.

So how do you build a castle? One stone on top of the other. One goal at a time. The good news is that there has never been a better time than today to build an online business. Multi-billion dollar companies are launching new tools for entrepreneurs each day, things like Instagram and Pinterest. They launch tools that either didn't exist or that you would have had to pay a lot of money to use as little as ten years ago. Now you can leverage those companies' investments in technology to build your own business.

Chapter Two Q&A with Cinnamon:

Jason: What would you say is the most important goal for a new craft business entrepreneur to focus on?

Cinnamon: Obviously the goal is to have your item sell. I think a lot of people focus on quantity instead of quality. They don't invest the time to make something really well and have really good pictures. Buyers on Etsy or eBay scroll through listings, so you have to make it your goal to create things that stand out. So for me, the number one goal is to produce really high-quality work. Then let the customer decide how much to pay for it through an auction.

Jason: So do you focus on how long it takes you to make a new outfit, or just on the quality you're trying to achieve?

Cinnamon: At this point, I can justify the time involved in creating a new outfit, which usually takes me a few weeks to figure out, because I'm confident it will sell for a high price and the patterns will be sold later.

Jason: What was your original inspiration for making your outfits?

Cinnamon: I'm a visual person, so whenever I see something that inspires me, I usually think, *I can make that.* Or, *How did they make that?* So my inspiration is not about making the business, it's about making exciting designs. When we first started, we were seeing a lot of Hannah Montana iron-on t-shirts for dolls. They did fit well, but they weren't interesting and exciting. So I thought, *Why not make the actual outfit that Hannah Montana is wearing?* The girls in that demographic wanted to pretend their doll was Hannah Montana, not a fan wearing a t-shirt.

Jason: What about after Liberty Jane was up and going, did any companies impress you?

Cinnamon: After we started doing auctions, I remember hearing about Keepers Dolly Duds and how the company sold its items for over $100. We were selling ours for between $40 and $50, so it was pretty inspiring. The owner's attention to detail and position in the market were really impressive. She specialized in historical clothing, which wasn't what I was interested in doing, but I did aspire to that high level of quality and selling power. I had no idea there was a community of collectors that were looking for high-end collectible clothes. Originally I thought it was a toy market, not a collectors market. So at that point, I changed my approach and the goal was to gain a respected position in our niche and a fan following. Knowing that my doll clothes would be considered collectible display items also changed what I was willing to make. Making a keepsake is a lot different than making an expensive toy item.

Day #2 Action Step: Take your journal and write down a financial goal for your small business. Don't worry about how you're going to achieve it just yet. Simply focus on a clear monthly goal. Our original goal was $1,000 a month. For a sewing and selling business, that is achievable. It might be a stretch, but it is achievable. We'll show you how. Additionally, if you want to really improve your odds of success, and you're married, talk to your spouse about this topic. If you can convince your spouse to help you build your business, then you'll do even better. But even if they aren't interested in helping, if they support the goal and understand how it will help financially, they'll probably be much more supportive.

Day #3
The DSB Model

Fortunately, for any crafter there is a business model that is a well-worn path toward establishing a 'castle with an unbreachable moat.' It is a business model that has been used by the famous artists of the Renaissance as well as modern fashion designers. It works. And you can use it if you understand it.

We call it the Designer–Seller Business Model (the DSB Model). The idea is simple: establish yourself and your brand as a design leader in your category or subcategory, and sell direct to the public.

Most people think that to be successful at a craft business, you have to 'make a good product and sell it at a fair price.' But that will never be enough to create a profitable long-term business. Why not? Because there is always someone willing to make something as good as you can, and sell it for less money. So you need to build a brand or reputation in the market and get fans, followers, and customers. Building a profitable craft business means building a well-loved brand.

Warren Buffett talks a lot in his letters about the idea of a 'castle with an unbreachable moat' and other people have expanded on his thinking to clarify how a business can become bulletproof. And it is not hard for a craft business to apply these principles. Let me explain them briefly.

Brand: Your brand is your reputation in the marketplace. The stronger your brand power and the more widely known it is, the more money you will make compared to the competition. As I write this, we have an eBay auction running for an outfit named 'Euro Libby – Le Marais.' There is one day and eight hours left. There have been 16 bids and the current bid is $90. It has been viewed over 1,500 times. It will likely end with a final bid price over $150, maybe higher. That happens because we have a strong brand, and because it happens our brand gets stronger. It is a self-reinforcing loop.

Community: Your fans, followers, and customers — if you can keep them interested and engaged — become an incredibly important part of your long-term success. Everyone is worried about competition, but a better question is: How can I create a product to turn my competition into my customer? How can I make them part of a community? We learned this lesson in the fall of 2009, when we launched Liberty Jane Patterns. Creating a community is much smarter than creating competitors.

Ecosystem: Remember the Corridor Principle?

The beautiful part of that idea is the realization that in any niche or sub-niche, there are multiple ways to make money. Some ideas are better than others. But if you think carefully about how to grow, you can end up with a nice collection of self-supporting products and programs. Those products are like an ecosystem. Our ecosystem includes the following: design work, auctions, pattern publishing, physical products, e-books, websites that we run which other people can publish on (both LibertyJanePatterns.com and Dollabee.com), online classes and membership sites, and even money from advertising.

In many ways, all of this is possible if you can design well and become a leader in your niche or sub-niche. But you're going to tell me that you're not talented enough to be considered a top designer in your niche, right? Don't worry; I'm prepared to convince you that you can do this.

Here are my arguments:

1. There is a continuum of originality that exists in any craft, and to be an amazing designer does not mean you have to be completely original. We've done very well by having Cinnamon reinterpret current tween clothing into the doll space. Are there opportunities in your niche to do something similar? Is there a style that is missing? That simple strategy alone can get you through the first few years of your new craft business.

2. For customers, a good brand name reinforces the impression that you are a professional designer. In fact, if you have an amazing brand, people will assume you are a good designer. Brands have power. When we get to Day #4, we'll look into the concept of building a professional brand.

3. Your reputation as a designer can gain momentum over time. Each successful auction or sales event provides an opportunity to elevate your status to a new and higher level. You can struggle for five years with mediocre results, but once you establish yourself as an elite provider, you rarely go backwards. And the faster you can position yourself as a premium provider, the faster your reputation will grow.

4. If you choose a small enough niche, you can become number one. Many people want to compete with a category leader in a large category. They think somehow the leader is making every product that customers could possibly want, in every way that customers could want it. That is simply wrong. We are in the age of what is called 'mass customization.' In your niche or sub-niche there is undoubtedly a small subcategory that has been left open for you to dominate. It is called a hole in the market. It might be a subcategory that no one has even thought of yet, which would allow you to become

the 'original.' Here is a good example from the doll patterns space: one of our pattern design partners, Meg, runs Miche Designs. After the success of our Janes shoe pattern, she proposed doing more doll shoe patterns in lots of varieties. No one was doing it. She clearly saw it as an open opportunity. Now she is crushing it in that new sub-niche. She is building a solid reputation for her excellent doll shoe patterns. Her patterns are popular and customers are asking for more and more.

How does the Designer–Seller Business Model work? Let's walk through the model so you understand how to use it.

Step 1: Identify a unique approach to your niche, or a sub-niche that is available for you to dominate. Cinnamon's unique approach was to make 'on-trend' clothing for American Girl dolls. The unique approach might be very subtle, but it needs to be clear to you.

A unique approach to your niche can really be anything that is not currently done well, but that *you* can do well. You want to find a hole in the market. Look at your niche, take one specific aspect of it, and become the 'specialist' in that specific thing. Being unique might include things like:

- unique color palettes
- uncommon material choices, like vintage

fabrics
- fun trends applied to your niche, like steampunk
- minimalism
- ultra-rare materials
- unique packaging or presentation
- combining two popular design styles
- going ultra-modern if people are doing historical
- going historical if people are going modern

What is important to realize is that your unique approach does not have to be as fundamental as the actual design of the items. It could be how you put it together or a certain design feature. As you focus on your niche, you'll find that many options open up. The main thing is to position your products as unique so they stand out.

Step 2: Publish items rarely, or in a special way. Creating a Spring and Fall Line, a limited edition set of 10 items, or a one-of-a-kind outfit is always better than simply cranking out 20 copies of the same item. It is more work to spend five hours on one item, and then to auction it, than it is to spend one hour on a simple item and sell it for $20. By launching your items in a unique or special way, you add a whole collection of positive selling factors that will help you be successful in selling. Your reputation, in part, is built on the prices you're able to achieve for your items. When you list your items on Etsy and they sell out in 10 minutes, people notice. Or, if you list your product at auction and it goes for an ultra-premium price, people notice. You want people to notice. The best way for that to happen is to make selling your items a big event. We'll cover that in detail in Day #15.

Step 3: Work on your brand, not just on your products. Ultimately, your brand is the real asset that you are working to build, and your individual product sales are the proof that it is growing stronger. We'll focus more on creating a brand in the next chapter. But needless to say, a solid personal brand adds huge power.

Step 4: Obsess over the photography, copywriting, and overall presentation of your items. Great brands are presented in a great ways. They are always photographed well, and the writing associated with their products is compelling. Your brand is influenced more by your photography, writing, and presentation than it is by the actual 'quality' of your work. I realize this is hard to accept, but it is true. Quality is important, but quality presentation is in many ways more important. And yes, we'll work on photography and copywriting in the upcoming chapters.

Step 5: Be a student of design, trends, and shifting consumer tastes. The best designers constantly redefine, reinterpret, and reposition their collections as 'trendy,' even when the trends change. And once you start serving customers in a specific niche, you'll learn how tastes change and how best to change with the times.

Chapter Three Q&A with Cinnamon:

Jason: How important do you think branding is to our success?

Cinnamon: From the very first item we put online, we had a very strong brand. I think it gave the impression that we were bigger than just me sitting at the dining room table sewing on my old Kenmore sewing machine.

Jason: Do you consider your designs original?

Cinnamon: Original is a funny word, I guess. I don't think there are any original designs anywhere. There are only so many ways you can wear clothes. I like to copy what I see on a person and apply it to doll clothes because it is not in the doll space. I don't ever look at doll clothes and try to copy them. I take pictures of people who walk by me in the mall and I think, *I should make that dress*. Then I tweak it and make it work for what I'm doing. So it never comes out like an actual copy. Even when I was doing Hannah Montana outfits, it was never the exact same thing. It was just enough to make people realize what I was doing.

Jason: Do you get mad when people copy your designs?

Cinnamon: Now that we are selling patterns, I can't blame them. The only time it ever bothers me is when I see the wholesale manufacturers out of China copying my items. In a way it is flattering, I guess. My hope with the patterns is that people will use them, but have enough creative inspiration to make them into their own unique items. Some people do that well; other people aren't wired that way and they make the exact same version.

Jason: What would say to someone struggling to find their own unique design style?

Cinnamon: Keep trying. Trust your instincts. Don't be afraid to try something new. Some of my best selling things were items that I liked but that my daughters didn't like. But I just went ahead and made it the way I liked it. That was the case with our U.K. Holiday outfit. It was the first outfit I sold for over $100. To be unique, you have to trust your instincts. You can't just copy what is already out there in your space.

Jason: What would you say to someone who is in a very competitive space?

Cinnamon: I would focus on the packaging, the logo, and the display. On eBay or Etsy, you have a sea of 1-inch by 1-inch pictures and you've got to find a way to stand out. It needs to be strikingly simple.

Day #3 Action Step: Take your journal and write down unique approaches to your niche that you think might be successful. Make a list of the possible options than come to mind, and prioritize them based on your interests, skills, and best guesses about what will stand out and generate enthusiasm in the marketplace.

Day #4

B Is for Brand

Brands can have real power. As we've discussed in prior chapters, your ultimate goal is to produce amazing products that strengthen your reputation in the marketplace. Your brand, whether it is your name or a company name, will absorb that positive energy, and in people's minds you'll earn your spot amongst their favorite companies. But to do it right, you've got to set up your brand concept properly. Let's look at 10 elements that will help you get it right.

Choose a unique name. When choosing a potential name, consider using your name or a unique proper name that has few or no similar results when entered in a search engine. In other words, choose something that you think is unique and use Google to confirm it. It's not impossible — keep trying, because if you fail to do this, you'll be sorry. Wouldn't you be horrified if you found out later that your fun new name was already associated with something yucky, gross, morbid, or totally inappropriate?

Go abstract. If you're not going to use a proper

name, then instead of trying to be 'cute,' go for something rather meaningless (Old Navy is one example). This is counterintuitive, but you don't want a brand name to have very much mental or emotional 'baggage' when you start your business. That way you can convey the deep meaning of your brand elements over time, and in people's minds those elements will become the prominent memory instead of any built-in implications. If you use generic words, it's like trying to stake a claim on a spot in your prospect's mind that they've already assigned to someone else; you cannot have it.

Avoid using the category as a default portion of your name. 'So and So's Doll Clothes' — if you use that name, you've used two generic words in your business's name, and you want to avoid generic words because they'll never be associated with your brand. You cannot have them in your prospect's minds; they are permanently muddled. They are associated with the concept or the category — not good. As a side note, lots of the 'mommy coupon bloggers' are getting this all wrong right now. They are tacking on the category words in the hope that they'll be remembered, but just the opposite happens. The entire category is growing and some will be winners, but it will probably be the ones with the strongest brands. As I'm trying to think of an example, the one that comes to mind is (uniquely named) 'Northern Cheapskate.' No 'mommy' or 'coupon' anywhere in there. And that is part of the reason why I remembered it.

Create deep meaning. Don't just choose a name. Choose a name that conveys attributes that are helpful to your cause. Attributes that reinforce what you're trying to convey to the world. Nike means champion. That's cool, right? 'Northern Cheapskate' makes it sound like the writers aren't New Yorkers or from La-La Land. They must be from someplace cold, harsh, rural, and frugal. Deep meaning. When we were brainstorming the name for our little company, we knew that it needed to relate to American Girl in some way. We kicked around lots of names, then realized our daughter's name fit perfectly (at least we think it does). It conveys Americana. It does that because she was born around 9/11 and we were feeling particularly patriotic back then, so we deliberately chose a name that felt 'American' when we named her. In fact, we considered naming her 'America' at the time. Years later, we were looking for a good brand name to support the American Girl ecosystem and the stars aligned around 'Liberty Jane.' Deep meaning.

Clarify your brand attributes. What do you want people to remember about you? Boil it down. Boil it down to one word if you can. Then try to have that word reinforced by everything you do. But here is the critical part: the attribute must be available right now in the minds of the consumer. It can't just be what you want to be, it has to be what your customer can appreciate, recall, and attach to your brand—ideally what they want and cannot find. Our brand's words are 'trendy' and 'exclusive.' They're our guiding light.

Brand attributes don't just say what you ARE about, they also say what you AREN'T about. If we're trendy and exclusive, how could we compete on price or sell on Amazon? Nope, not exclusive enough. If we're trendy, how can we do historical outfits? Nope, not trendy enough.

Go small when choosing a niche. If you're still reading this and you're thinking that all the good attributes are already taken, then there is one simple trick you need to consider: think narrow and deep. In every category (as you search on Amazon or eBay, for example), there are category leaders. But part of the power of Internet marketing is that if you want to own a single attribute and become known for it, there is almost endless open territory available for a good solid brand.

Pick the right price point for your brand. New customers have an amazing sorting function in their brain and the first filter is price. You will either be thrown into the expensive or inexpensive bucket. It doesn't matter if you don't like it; that's how it works. Companies spend millions of dollars trying to manage their way around this or convey deeper attributes of their brand, but most successful brands are very clear about this fundamental issue. They've chosen to go either high or low. Staying in the middle is a hard place to live as a brand.

Be real. If you're going to be an exclusive artisan, then don't act bigger than you are or overly corporate. People buy from people. Your brand, after getting a high or low price tag in the minds of prospects, will get a 'cool' or 'uncool' tag. And the single most important element in getting a 'cool' vote is authenticity. Be authentic. Tell your story. Have a really nice picture taken. Present yourself in the best light possible, both for the picture and the overall message. You don't have to be young and pretty to be considered cool. Just be yourself. The important part to understand here is that once people see your brand and answer the 'high' or 'low' question, then they'll start to judge you on the merits of what you've presented and they'll quickly make a determination about whether you're 'cool' or 'uncool.' In *Focus: The Future of Your Company Depends on It*, Al Reis says that:

> *"Somewhere in the corner of the prospect's brain there is a penalty box for brands they decide are losers."*

Don't be in that box.

Polish it up. Nowadays, there is no reason you can't have a professional looking logo. Try Elance if you want to hire somebody. You'd be surprised how fast, easy, and inexpensive it can be. That's who we used—actually it was some kid in the U.K. named 'Razor' and he did a great job on our logos. Another route to take is using Fiverr, a website that lists lots of jobs that people are willing to do for $5. Logo work is a very popular category.

Don't be afraid to change! If you need to change your name because it's not effective, don't be afraid to do it. If you do it carefully and systematically so customers are along for the ride, you won't lose anything and you'll gain a lot. So don't stress if you realize you need to make a change.

Chapter Four Q&A with Cinnamon:

Jason: What common mistakes do you see when you look at brands?

Cinnamon: I think people get stuck on names that are too close to what they are selling. Like 'My Sock Shop', or 'Somebody's Doll Clothes'. But a unique name like Poppy Parker or Maiden Flight is more unique and memorable. I know you can change your name if it's not right, but you don't want to change it into a name that isn't any better.

Jason: Did you have any other brand names before you settled on Liberty Jane Clothing?

Cinnamon: We brainstormed a lot and settled on Liberty Jane Clothing, using our daughter's name. We thought that was original until we started to get into it more and realized tons of people use their daughters' names for their businesses. But Liberty Jane has worked pretty well for us.

Jason: Did you realize how important branding

would be for the company?

Cinnamon: I'm not a brander. I make the outfits. You're the one that understood this before I did. Now I understand how important it is, but at the beginning I didn't.

Jason: Stories and descriptions are a big part of your outfits. What comes first, the outfit or the story?

Cinnamon: The outfit, sort of. The signature pieces come first. Then we decide which of the four themes — Euro Libby, Outback Libby, Tokyo Libby, or Malibu Libby — the items might work well with. Then I complete the outfit to go with that theme. Then the name and the story are last. Usually after I make the outfit I say to you, "please come make up a name and a story for this outfit." I think most people would be surprised that you do that part. I'm not a storyteller.

Day #4 Action Step: Brainstorm your brand names and choose five that you like. Then ask your spouse, children, or friends for their feedback. Google your favorite ideas to check for other instances of the name then go to GoDaddy.com and search to see if it is available as a domain name. If not, then move on to your second choice or an available variation of your first choice. Once you settle on a name, purchase the domain on GoDaddy.com or a similar site.

Day #5

Decision Day

It is time to pick a 'go-to-market' product. Review your list from Day #3 and decide which one of the products is your best bet for your business launch.

To launch a product successfully, you've got to find your unique angle or idea — and it needs to be a popular one. If you offer a unique product that is in line with the desires of the marketplace, then you've got a great shot at building a good business.

You see, selling is a balancing act between offering something uniquely new and offering what is already popular in the marketplace.

But don't worry about failing. Sometimes it's impossible to know what people are going to find attractive, but it's your job to experiment until you get it right. Sometimes you have an idea and it flops. Sometimes you have an idea and it works like magic. Don't be discouraged by the flops, and don't become complacent with the wins. You'll want to keep learning and keep moving forward.

It's tricky. On the one hand, if you just copy what other people are doing, even if it's selling well for them, then you haven't differentiated yourself enough to get people's attention. You might do okay, but probably not great. Over time, your lack of distinctiveness will diminish your ability to stand out and make a lot of money.

On the other hand, if you deviate from what's popular too much, you run the risk of making products that look goofy and unattractive. Goofy usually doesn't sell well. Your taste matters tremendously.

The best approach is to be unique enough to stand out, but to stick to concepts that are known winners. Find a crowd of people who wants something and give it to them in a unique and fun way.

So how do you decide?

Here are three proven ideas inspired by Paul Hawken, founder of Smith & Hawken and author of *Growing a Business*:

Take the ultra-premium provider spot. Most craft business owners assume that 'homemade' needs to mean 'lower-priced.' That is not true. In fact, most success stories you hear are about artisans positioning themselves as ultra-premium providers. They take the high-price, low-volume route.

Here is our example: when we entered the doll clothes category on eBay in 2008, there were several types of clothing being sold. Almost all the expensive couture clothes focused on the 'historical clothing' subcategory (for the collector community). That subcategory had three pricing tiers:

1. Low-priced providers, which included both mass-manufactured stuff from China and sew-from-home sellers.

2. Expensive providers, which is where American Girl dominated.

3. Ultra-premium providers, where a few very popular sellers had made a name for themselves.

Cinnamon was not interested in the historical clothing subcategory, however she was very interested in contemporary design. So she began making couture clothes focused on trendy designs in the 'contemporary clothes' subcategory.

In that category, almost all of the competitors were selling items for less than the category leader, American Girl. Sellers included mass manufacturers and sew-from-home providers. At the time, American Girl clothes were thought to be as expensive as anyone would possibly be willing to pay.

So by creating insanely great designs and running

everything as one-of-a-kind or limited edition auctions, we were able to become one of the only 'ultra-premium' providers in that subcategory. We effectively repositioned the 'trendy clothing' subcategory into three pricing tiers. The three tiers became:

1. Low cost providers, which is where 98% of the competitors chose to compete. What they fail to realize is that there is always someone willing to sell for less than them, and it becomes a price war that destroys everyone in that part of the market.

2. Expensive providers, which is where American Girl dominates.

3. Ultra-premium providers, which is where we've established ourselves.

Can you reposition the category or subcategory leader in your niche to become the new ultra-premium provider?

Reveal a business-within-a-business. Maybe there are subcategories that have not yet been defined. Take one small area of your niche and focus on it with a level of intensity, quality, and marketing skill that blows customers away. You are taking a gamble that you can actually find a hungry crowd of buyers eager to support your new vision, but if you validate that there are eager buyers, you'll have a great new business opportunity. You limit your universe and dominate it by doing it in a very professional way.

Have you ever heard of Charles Williams? He was a simple hardware store owner. In 1956, he decided to get rid of all the hardware and just focus on one small subcategory that no one else was focused on at the time. His new subcategory? Kitchen utensils. You probably love Williams-Sonoma, his now famous store. He found success by defining a new subcategory and then fully serving that market in a professional and interesting way. Become the best at one small thing.

Revitalize abandoned product lines. Is there something in your area of interest that no one else is doing? Or something that another company abandoned? It may not be because there is not customer demand. Big companies are required to justify very large sales volume in a subcategory to make it a profitable revenue line, so they might abandon ideas that are perfect for a smaller provider.

When we decided to launch Liberty Jane Patterns into the doll clothes sewing subcategory, we knew that the American Girl Company had created six patterns many years before and had clearly abandoned that line of business. They were paper patterns, but the digital revolution had changed how patterns could be made and sold. For more than 20 years, no one took advantage of this hole in the marketplace, either offline or online. Additionally, the very large pattern companies did not have a robust collection of patterns in the doll space. It was a minor footnote in their collections.

It was like a vast territory had been abandoned by American Girl and neglected by the big pattern companies. So we decided we'd enter that space and offer the largest selection of doll clothes patterns we could possibly create, delivering them via digital download. Three years later, we have over 200 patterns and have had them downloaded over 200,000 times. We weren't competing with American Girl; we were adding something of value to their ecosystem.

Finally, remember that your packaging is part of the product experience. You can build customer loyalty and enthusiasm by really taking the time to make your packaging interesting and fun. When you label products as handmade by an artisan, that's a lot different than homemade. Make your packaging great.

Chapter Five Q&A with Cinnamon:

Jason: Some people might find it hard to find a unique niche. What advice would you give?

Cinnamon: Sometimes it's sitting right in front of you. I made the doll clothes for the girls, and the moms at the dance studio wanted to buy them. Brian, our brother-in-law, was in the airplane maintenance business and had old parts lying around. He thought, *Hey, would people buy these old parts if I cleaned them up and made them into functional art?* I think people would be surprised to realize there are collectors for almost every type of item. So it comes down to being proud of your work, listing it like a professional, having great pictures, and making it seem like it should be highly sought after.

Jason: What do you think the most important part of a product launch is?

Cinnamon: Taking the time to launch it really well. Sometimes you finish it and just want to turn it around and put it up for sale. But you need to build up the anticipation and hype, especially if it is a seven-day auction. You want to make sure that lots of people are aware that you're going to list it.

Jason: Do you ever worry that you're going to make something that really doesn't click with buyers?

Cinnamon: Not anymore. I'm always slightly anxious before people start to bid on our auctions. You wonder if anyone cares. But at this point, we have a large enough crowd that we can appeal to different people's interests. Not everybody will like everything.

Jason: Do you think it's better to have a broad line of items in a niche, or to focus on one specific thing that you can become known for?

Cinnamon: It's hard to tell sometimes. Williams-Sonoma focused on the kitchen, but not the fork. When I'm at Williams-Sonoma I think, *I can get this stuff at Target*, but it's not as fun to shop at Target for kitchen items. Sometimes you have a signature item, like the Coach Purse, but then you sell other items. It's good to focus on a style or concept, like contemporary, historical, or steampunk. Sometimes in fashion you can do homage and do really well. That is how I started with the Hannah Montana items. But then I realized I could sell my own items just as well.

Day #5 Action Step: Finalize your product decision and the unique way in which you're going to sell it. Write your decision boldly in your journal. The rest of this e-book will focus on how to successfully launch that product.

Day #6

Crowd-Sourced Prices

If you are making handmade goods, then you are selling something called a rival good. Economists talk about the idea of rival versus non-rival goods. It sounds fancy, but it's really pretty simple.

A rival good is one that people have to fight over if they want it, because there is a limited supply (a rivalry occurs). Examples include:

- the Hope Diamond
- a Picasso painting
- 12 slices of pizza sitting in front of a hungry football team

When a rival good is up for auction and it has a strong perceived value in people's minds, people fight, prices escalate, winners win, and losers lose. People immediately recognize that scarcity will create competition for the item.

A non-rival good is one that has infinite supply. Examples include:

- Liberty Jane digitally downloaded patterns

- iTunes songs
- broadcast TV

Any digitally delivered product falls into this category unless someone is artificially controlling supply. When you're shopping for a non-rival good, there is no need to rush; there is enough for everyone because there is an endless supply. There is no rivalry amongst the buyers. If you want it, you buy it, and there are still an infinite number of 'copies' available for the next person.

Mass manufacturing has blurred the lines between these two ideas. There are a finite number of iPhones; it is a rival good, but they've made so many that they can act like it is a non-rival good when they decide on pricing. This is pretty much true for any mass-manufactured item. Companies sometimes manipulate this deliberately by making a finite number of each design, and then escalating the price and creating perceived scarcity (think Porsche). But for most mass-manufactured items, there are plenty of copies available.

Pricing Principle 1: Fixed prices are appropriate for non-rival goods because there is enough for everyone, no need to fight, and no opportunity for sellers to profit from the rivalry.

In addition to companies manipulating this deliberately, occasionally this system of 'non-rival fixed pricing' breaks down. We realize this when a product is so popular that it outpaces manufacturing. When Apple releases a cool new product and they only make 3 million, but a lot of people want one, what happens? You see them on eBay for crazy prices because some smart marketer has identified the fact that with a shortage of supply, there is an opportunity to get higher prices.

Pricing Principle 2: Auctions are appropriate for rival goods because there is not enough for everyone and there is an opportunity to profit from the rivalry.

As a seller of rival goods, the best selling strategy is an auction format if you have a good product and can attract a crowd. Why? Because you acknowledge that there are more people that want the item than there are items, and the only fair way to settle it is through an auction: a crowd-sourced price.

The wisest selling strategy for a non-rival good is a fixed price, because there is no concern in anyone's mind about scarcity. You just set a reasonable price and let the market decide about the popularity. If it's not popular, you end up discounting until people see it as a good value.

If you have a rival good and your selling strategy is to act like it's a non-rival good, you're failing to use scarcity when you legitimately should.

If you're making 18-inch doll clothes, then think about this: are you pricing your items at the same level as American Girl? They have an almost infinite supply; you only have a few. Shouldn't you take advantage of this scarcity? If you price it the same as the Chinese imports and try to sell it in the same way (with a fixed 'buy it now' pricing strategy), you're making a mistake.

If you can make your product well and attract a following, you should use auctions to help create a sense of rivalry and competition and then use that to establish your premium prices. That's been our approach at Liberty Jane, and it works.

As our partners have implemented this approach, it has worked for them, too. Manage the scarcity. Don't lie about anything — you don't have to — just be honest. You can only make a limited number of handmade, hand-carved, or hand-painted items in your home or studio. You're not a Chinese factory. Make people realize that — and get paid what you're worth!

Pricing Principle 3: There are real forces that work to undermine and erode your premium pricing. You have to be willing to fight those forces. You have to be willing to stand your ground. This is not about earnings as much as it is about your mindset and your determined point of view.

As Malcolm X once said,

> *"Nobody can give you freedom. Nobody can give you equality or justice or*

anything. If you're a man, you take it."

If you'll allow us to adapt this to pricing, we might say:

> *"Nobody wants to pay a premium price, or pay what things are worth, or what you're asking. It's your job to make them."*

So we recommend you auction your items to establish premium prices, then use those results to justify a high price for your 'buy it now' items.

In an auction:

- We aren't setting the price; the crowd is in charge of that.
- No one can complain and tell us to lower our prices.
- The final bid price of your outfit sets the stage for your next auction. The last auction-ending price is frequently the 'new floor.'
- When your auction ends high, it validates your pricing. Why would anyone expect you to make a custom piece for $30 when your item sells at auction for over $300?

Chapter Six Q&A with Cinnamon

Jason: Your auctions are starting to frequently end above $200. With your best auction ending at $335, do you think they will continue to go higher?

Cinnamon: I don't know — I guess that's the fun of doing the auction format. The $335 was the final item of our Spring 2012 line, but the first item for our Fall 2012 line was just $86. So there is a huge range that seems possible.

Jason: Can you predict which outfits are going to sell for more money than others, or is it a mystery?

Cinnamon: Some outfits come together really well and there isn't just one primary piece, like a jacket, that has all the detail and complexity. In those outfits, all the other pieces stand out as well. Each piece is unique. Those tend to be the ones that go for the highest prices. When I make outfits that include a pair of jeans and a t-shirt, it's hard to expect it to go for a top amount.

Jason: Do you ever feel like there are items that are under-appreciated and don't sell well?

Cinnamon: Sometimes items look very simple, but they're not. Recently, I did the Tokyo Libby Snow Club dress. It was just a tank style dress, but it had really nice fabric and it was lined and constructed like a real dress, just like one you'd find at Nordstrom. But it looked simple on the doll. So I tried to show the details through the photography and the description. But it's tricky — you don't want to go on and on about how it took you six hours to install the zipper — people sort of get tired of that.

Jason: Has the crowd ever let you down?

Cinnamon: Yep, one time. It was in 2009. One of my outfits sold for just $8.49. That was painful. But we learned from it and of course the customer was ecstatic. There was simply no one else there to bid against her, so she got an amazing deal. There was a period of time when I had a numbered set of outfits that I would list sporadically. So people wouldn't know when to show up and bid for the outfit they wanted. We didn't forecast our plan well enough to our customers.

Jason: Was there any silver lining in that situation beyond the lesson of not being sporadic?

Cinnamon: It made us realize we always need a well-communicated plan for when we are selling. It also let our existing customers know that if they show up and bid, they might get an amazing deal. It sort of acts as a long-term incentive for the bargain hunters. They show up to each auction now to see if they can get a deal.

Day #6 Action Step: Research auctioning your items on eBay. Visit the Liberty Jane Clothing store on eBay and see how we've listed items previously. Find examples of exceptional auctions. See how they used photography, copywriting, and other elements to maximize revenue. If you can create an auction listing that draws dramatic bidding and high final bid prices, then you are well on your way to success. It will take good photography, good copywriting, and a well-created product.

Day #7

Sell Everything You Make

We strongly recommend selling items via eBay auctions. Auctioning your items is the easiest way to establish an ultra-premium price for your products. The truth is that there is a very broad range of prices that are possible for the same item. The auction format is the only way to easily maximize the price you can achieve. Once your high prices are established in the marketplace through auctions, it becomes easier to charge premium prices for your 'buy-it-now' items.

Our practice is to run eBay auctions two times a year. We work hard to make these auctions a really big event. These auctions are the way in which we sell our Spring Line and our Fall Line. They represent the highlight of our selling efforts in any given year.

<u>Five Reasons Auctions Have So Much Power:</u>

Anchoring: Anchoring is a psychological concept that affects buyer behavior.

People cannot forget about relevant (and even irrelevant) numbers and prices related to your offer and those prices will affect their decisions. For 18-inch doll clothes, it is the American Girl prices — their outfits are sold for $39. That price point is the anchor that buyers are attached to. You cannot price higher than AG without overcoming several challenges. Their prices are an anchor.

The anchor can also work within your own shop and in your favor. Prada uses the anchoring strategy very wisely. They place a $300 purse next to a $2,400 purse. In that context, the $300 purse seems like a bargain. When you run an auction and achieve ultra-premium prices, you are able to employ this same strategy. So anchors have to be used to help you and not hurt you.

Earnings: If you're going to make an item, why sell it for $19 when you can auction it and get a lot more? The math works better via auctions. This difference should not be overlooked. If you can sell an item via auction for three times more than you could sell it at a fixed-price, then the following are all true:

- You can work a third of the time and make the same money as you would selling items at fixed prices.
- You can sell the same number of items and make three times as much money.
- Your hourly wage goes up by three times.
- The perceived value of your work is much

higher.

Complaining: In our category, our biggest issue with selling fixed-priced items is that people are intensely focused on the AG anchor prices, so if you try to list your items higher than AG's, then you have a constant flow of customer feedback with one request — *"lower your prices"*. What are they saying? They're saying, "Hey, in my head, I have a number, and your price is too much higher than that number, so I'm unhappy with you." Unfortunately, oftentimes people make this comment in public places almost as a way to scold you. So you're compelled to argue or defend your prices. It's a hassle. If you had a private counter at Neiman Marcus, then you could get away with high fixed-priced items, because no one would shout, "NO WAY!" But this isn't Neiman Marcus; this is the Internet.

So when someone complains about high prices, you can't say, "Hey look, this took me 15 hours to make, and I used material that cost four times more than the material anyone else uses, and I designed the pattern from scratch, and unless I want to pay myself a dollar an hour, I need to sell it for more than $19 bucks."

Scarcity: The nature of an auction is that there is one item available and many people want it. This is referred to as scarcity. It is a fundamental economic problem: too many people and not enough items. People react very consistently when they are confronted with a scarcity situation. They become greedy and obsessed. This emotional response energizes people to participate in the auction.

Urgency: Deadlines produce action. When customers know that the auction is ending at 6:00 PM and someone is going to win the item, they become very focused. People are forced to decide how much they are willing to bid and if they even want the item at all.

How to Get the Most out of eBay Auctions:

Starting at 99 Cents: Anything will sell on eBay if you start it at 99 cents. The real question is not whether you can sell what you make; it is if you can get a price you think you deserve. If there is a market, and you list it on eBay for 99 cents, you'll end up with a sale. The reason a 99 cents starting point is important is because it engages the maximum number of people. If your auction lingers at just a few dollars, people get emotionally invested in the idea of getting it for a bargain. They get their heart set on the item.

Using a Listing Template: The listing templates in eBay give your auction a level of quality that is well worth the ten cents. Choosing a listing template that is thematically relevant to your auction creates the perception that you've made something very special.

Including a Subtitle: By paying an additional 50 cents, you get the option of including a subtitle for your auction. The ability to include this additional information can be very valuable. In our view, it is well worth the cost.

Including Embedded Photography: Having your images hosted on a photo-sharing site and included in the body of your eBay listing allows you to have very large, prominent pictures of your items. This is in addition to uploading photos as part of the listing function. We use Photobucket as our image-hosting tool. There are tutorials online that demonstrate how to do this simply.

Using Image Gallery Plus: You can upload 12 photos as part of the eBay listing function. You should fully utilize this functionality and also pay the extra charge (currently 35 cents) for the capability of enlarging your images when the customer hovers over them. Additionally, you'll want to ensure that your best picture is the first image in the gallery, so that it is the one prospective customers see while browsing.

Including Embedded Video: By taking your photos and uploading them to a site like Animoto, you can create a professional-looking video with a nice music soundtrack and high quality editing. The video can also be embedded in your YouTube listing.

Using a Money Back Guarantee: Rather than saying, 'All sales are final' we say, 'If you're not completely satisfied, we'll provide a full refund.' This strong promise reassures customers that you can be trusted to do the right thing, that you're guaranteeing them complete happiness with your product.

Being Consistent: We always have our auctions end on Sunday evening around 6:00 PM. This routine helps existing customers 'know the deal' and understand how we do it.

In addition to running these special auctions, we also sell items at fixed prices on our website. Our auctions give us the proof we need to list our fixed-priced items for premium prices. If you don't have a website to sell on directly, then Etsy is a good alternative for your fixed-priced items. Many sellers have abandoned eBay because of the high fees, but in our view, that is a very big mistake. An auction has many benefits that you just cannot get anywhere else.

How to Get the Most out of Fixed-Priced Items:

Batches: By selling items in small batches, you can introduce the emotional trigger of scarcity into the situation. If customers know there are only 10 items available, it prompts action. Small batches also help you gauge customer enthusiasm. If your first batch sells out instantly, then your next batch might need to be at a higher price point. On the other hand, if your items don't sell quickly, then maybe you need to modify the design or lower your prices.

Pre-Launch Information: As we'll cover in the

Product Launches chapter (Day #14), make sure that you are letting prospective buyers know what you're working on and when it will be available. This simple communication effort can radically impact your results. By previewing your items and sharing information ahead of time, you are pre-selling the items. Then customers will immediately get one when it becomes available.

Involving Customers: Asking your customers questions like, "Which color should my next batch of jeans be?" gets people engaged in the process and allows you to appeal to a group of ready buyers. You ask them what they want, and then you don't even really have to ask them to buy it; you just let them know when it is being listed.

Big companies spend thousands of hours testing price points. They do all sorts of complicated analyses, just to determine what the market will be for a certain item. What they find is that it is highly random and depends on many variables. There is no single price that is perfect. As an artisan, you don't need to do any of that work. You can let the market decide by effectively running auctions.

Chapter Seven Q&A with Cinnamon:

Jason: What are your thoughts on your eBay strategy?

Cinnamon: I love the idea of the customers setting the prices. Fixed-priced items are just so problematic for us. People would say horrible things about us when we listed fixed-priced items at high price points. But when we run auctions, people don't seem to have a problem. Plus, I like to not have to think about pricing. It's easier to just list it as an auction and let it go for what people are willing to pay. That way, you are placing your trust in the hands of your customers.

Jason: What are your thoughts on the 99 cents listing strategy?

Cinnamon: As an artist, it was very hard for me to believe in this approach. But you seemed passionate that it was the right way to go, in order to attract the interest of a wider range of bidders. I don't have a problem with it any more. We've done it so many times that I know we'll have bidders.

Jason: What are your thoughts on the high fees eBay charges?

Cinnamon: You have to go where the customers are and just factor it in. They have a business to run, and if you just accept it as part of the process, then it's not that bad. It's a good platform with millions of customers. But then again, we consider our auctions to be more promotional in nature than simply just a way to sell things. We consider it an event that helps generate interest in our work.

Day #7 Action Step: Plan your item production to ensure that you sell everything you make. Instead of scaling up production too soon, make a few variations that you can auction to determine customer enthusiasm. Create an auction so you get familiar with the listing template and how to use the additional features that will help your auction stand out.

Day #8

Click

Y ou cannot dominate your new niche with your cool new product if you cannot take exceptional pictures of it. A good picture conveys many important things about you, your brand, and your item, including:

- that you are a professional at what you are doing
- that the item is fantastic, because a fantastic picture helps show off the good qualities of the item
- that you have a commitment to high quality in both your photography and your product creation

Are these traits important to convey? Of course!

But it doesn't stop there.

Have you ever heard of the Halo Principle? It is an error in judgment that we all make. We generalize. And if we see some element of a 'thing' that is really amazing, we tend to think the whole thing will be amazing. We place a 'halo' on that item — and despite information to the contrary — in our eyes, it's amazing. Your customers do this each and every day, and they do it when looking at your products and your business.

But there is another side of the coin. The dark side.

What are the results of using bad photography in your listing? Well, here are a few:

- Customers think you're an amateur.
- Customers think you have low standards of quality.
- Customers think you have a dirty house and that you probably smoke or have 72 cats wandering around in your sewing room.

Are they interested in any of that? NO WAY! Too risky.

The generalizations go the other way, too. People tend to demonize or disrespect a seller unfairly based on just a few small issues, and photography is definitely one of them. So what should you do if you fear your pictures aren't up to the level of quality that your customers will respect?

It's pretty simple. You need to invest in a good camera.

I know, I know, you're trying to make money, not spend it, right? But in this case, you really cannot afford to operate without a good camera. You need a Digital Single Lens Reflex (DSLR) camera with a specific type of lens called a portrait lens. Not a point-and-shoot camera. If you're struggling with the quality of your pictures and you're using a point-and-shoot camera, you probably think you just don't know how to use it. The truth is that the lens used in a point-and-shoot camera will not deliver the kind of pictures that you need to do product photography.

But it takes more than a camera to take good pictures. It takes a certain eye, a way of seeing things, to take pictures that make people go "Wow!" Fortunately, this can be learned. And the more you practice, the better you'll get.

If you're interested in becoming a good digital photographer, start by taking a look at some of the most common mistakes people make when taking digital pictures:

Not Knowing Your Camera: If you never read

your digital camera's manual and learn it's features and how to use them, you won't be able to make the most of it. Of course, YouTube has tutorials on almost every possible type of camera. Search to see if there are tutorials that apply to your camera.

Taking Pictures Against the Light: This means having the light come from behind your object, rather than in front of the object. This makes the subject dark and the background too bright. You want to be outside in what is commonly referred to as open shade. Lighting your product well with natural light is the best possible tool you can use to take good pictures.

Relying Too Much on the Flash: Natural light produces the best pictures, so use it as much as possible. Flash tends to make images look harsh.

Not Taking Enough Pictures: It's almost impossible to take the perfect shot with one try, so take many pictures. With digital photography, this doesn't cost you extra. Try different angles and compositions.

Always Putting the Subject Dead Center: Learn the 'rule of thirds' in composition, and you'll have more interesting pictures. By placing your object off center, you add visual interest.

Forgetting to Check the Horizon: When taking pictures with the horizon showing, make sure it's level.

Selecting a Low-Resolution Setting: Your camera will allow you to select different resolutions. Don't be tempted to choose a low resolution just to save on memory space. Instead, buy additional memory for your camera and always take your pictures in high resolution.

Trying to Take Too Much: Don't try to include too many things in one picture, such as people and scenery. A picture is more effective when it's focused on a single subject.

Not Using the Camera Enough: Like any other trade skill, photography improvements come with practice.

Chapter Eight Q&A with Cinnamon:

Jason: How much of your success do you think is attributed to effective product photography?

Cinnamon: It is a huge part of what we've done. The photography was what made our very first listing on eBay stand out. If you shoot something like it's art rather than just a doll outfit, people take notice. When you use angles and composition to capture interesting details, you stand out in a crowded space.

Jason: What camera equipment do you use?

Cinnamon: I have a Canon 40D that I bought used on eBay for around $300. I have several lenses that I use, depending on the situation. Most of my product photography is shot with an 85 mm f/1.8 fixed length lens. I also frequently use a 30 mm f/1.4 lens.

Jason: What about lighting equipment?

Cinnamon: My preference is to shoot outside, which I can do in pretty much any light. We have a lot of nice open shade in our backyard. I use a simple tri-fold white foam core board for my background — the kind you would use for a science project and can get at most stores. I cut off one side so that it creates a seamless transition between the floor and the back. Frequently, I use the third part of the foam core that I cut off as a reflector to shine the sunlight back toward the product. People might be surprised that most of my shots are just on our back patio table. They look like studio images. I do have studio lighting that I use inside if the weather is particularly bad.

Jason: What do you do to the images after you've taken them?

Cinnamon: I like using Photoshop Elements to make simple edits. Cropping, white balance, and sharpening the images can help solve problems and add impact.

Jason: What mistakes do you see craft sellers commonly making?

Cinnamon: The most obvious are related to overall presentation. Messy or distracting backgrounds are a mistake. If it is a doll-related item, then having the doll's hair messy is something I always notice. Anything like that suggests to prospective buyers that the details aren't important to you. That's the wrong message to send. You want your photography to reinforce the idea that your item is professionally made.

Day #8 Action Step: Work on improving your photography. Take 100 pictures and look into purchasing a DSLR camera such as a Canon Rebel. Then look into purchasing a 50 mm portrait lens. You can buy both of these items secondhand on eBay for a few hundred dollars.

Day #9

Word

If you can substantially improve your product photography, then you've only got one other element of the product presentation that you need to master: copywriting. Copywriting can engage customers with your product in a compelling way, give them a reason to buy, and convince them that NOW is the best time to buy.

Good copywriting isn't fancy or even grammatically correct, but it is engaging. It provides a reason to buy. It provokes the customer's curiosity, then it satisfies it. It makes purchasing the product easy.

Here is an example: Not long ago, our daughter Libby started making doll clothes and selling them on Etsy. She wanted to do it all by herself. It was part of her 'I'm a big girl now' phase. So she didn't want Cinnamon to help her with the sewing activities or photography, nor did she want me to help her with the selling activities or copywriting. Fair enough.

We were excited by all of this and thought it was

amazing that she was taking the initiative; she's only 9. Good for her!

Her first listing was on Etsy in no time.

Trouble was . . . it didn't sell. She had taken a reasonably good picture, made a reasonably good outfit, listed it for a reasonable price, and written a reasonable description. Actually, it was all fairly good — better than some of the other items we regularly see on Etsy.

Finally, a little discouraged, Libby told me that she was frustrated, and asked for my help.

I made one simple change and her outfit sold within a day.

Can you guess what I did?

I went into her listing description and wrote the following sentences:

"I'm Liberty Jane Miles from Liberty Jane Clothing, you know, the doll clothes company? They named it after me, and this is my very first outfit I've ever made. I'm going to be a big designer someday, so if you want to be able to say you bought my very first outfit, then you should buy this outfit."

And — *Bam!* — it sold within a day.

So what did I actually do in those three sentences?

You know what I did, right? I used the power of a story. And with my story, I gave people a fun and interesting reason to buy her outfit. That story closed the deal. It wasn't manipulative or contrived; it was just a different angle on what was going on, which changed the customer's point of view. That got the reader interested in the item for a 'bigger' reason than just getting some new doll clothes.

Libby's buyer was now going to be part of a journey with Libby by investing in her future career as a designer. The story gave the buyer something to talk about with friends and family. It made the buyer consider the long-term impact of a seemingly simple buying decision.

These three sentences also take advantage of an important concept explained by Joe Sugarman, a master copywriter. He says,

> *"Never sell a product or service, always sell a concept."*

Wow. All that from three sentences?

Yep! That is the power of a story. The power of effective writing that sells.

So how can you write effectively to sell your outfits? Here are a few ideas:

1. Write clearly! Simple words. Simple sentences. Don't stress over elementary

school punctuation rules about writing.

2. Be complete. Take your time and consider all the good reasons that your customer should buy from you, and buy that particular product.

3. Use stories. Tap into your imagination to enhance the meaning and importance of your item.

   Ever heard of Malibu Barbie? Think about what its creators did. There is absolutely nothing that connects that doll to Malibu except the creative imagination that the marketer used when creating it, and then the clothes and accessories. In a similar way, Pleasant Roland was a master at using the power of stories, and built the American Girl doll brand on that simple idea.

   Starting last year, we launched our International Collection so we could do the same thing. It's been a fun and meaningful part of our work. Now we have Outback Libby, Euro Libby, and even Malibu Libby. Guess what? No one seemed to mind that we were taking a play straight from brands like Barbie and American Girl. It was different enough to be our own, but familiar enough to people that they enjoyed it.

   Can you come up with your own storyline?

4. Be concise. When you write, make sure that you take each idea, topic, or piece of information, and give it a unique paragraph. Separate elements using lists, bullet points, line breaks, or images to break your information up so it is easy to see and read. There is no need to cram everything into one gigantic paragraph. People won't read it.

One of the most powerful elements of copywriting is the use of emotional triggers to engage with prospects. In Joe Sugarman's book *The Adweek Copywriting Handbook*, he outlines them in detail. Here is part of his list:

- creating a feeling of involvement or ownership
- demonstrating honesty
- showing integrity
- credibility
- showing value and proof of value
- justifying the purchase
- greed (the customer's greed)
- establishing authority (your authority)
- satisfying their concerns through guarantees
- explaining the drama inherent within the product
- satisfying a desire to belong
- satisfying a desire to collect
- provoking curiosity
- creating a sense of urgency
- fear

- providing instant gratification
- explaining the product's exclusivity, rarity, or uniqueness
- storytelling
- guilt
- hope

Chapter Nine Q&A with Cinnamon

Jason: How do you approach copywriting for your products?

Cinnamon: For the most part, I rely your creative writing skills. I like to design and create, but not write. I feel like it's a joint venture. Sometimes we do it together, but frequently you do it.

Jason: Is there a company that has good copywriting that you enjoy?

Cinnamon: I like ModCloth's copy because it's fun — creative names, cute descriptions. We also have a stack of J. Peterman catalogs that we used to look at together a lot because we like their product descriptions.

Jason: What types of copywriting bother you? Why?

Cinnamon: I don't like copy that comes across as an infomercial or sales pitch. It doesn't seem genuine and feels like a pressure tactic. I feel like that is why it is nice to appeal to a collector market, because you can focus your presentation on the story and the details. In a collector market, you can appeal to people's sense of nostalgia and memories to help make a sale. It's a different kind of story.

Jason: Do you think the power of a story is the most important aspect of copywriting or is there something else?

Cinnamon: I guess if you look at someone's work, for example TOMS Shoes, you see an overall idea behind the entire product line. It's more than just a cute description. It's about the 'why.' That makes it more meaningful.

Jason: When you need to do the copywriting and create descriptions, what resources do you use?

Cinnamon: *Phrases That Sell* is a book I like a lot. There is a chapter on fashion. It gives you different ways of saying, "this cute dress," different phrases that describe an item or a style.

Day #9 Action Step: In your journal, write 20 sentences — one sentence for each of the 20 psychological triggers listed above. Apply each trigger to your product in a meaningful way. Think about how to effectively use these writing tools to position your product effectively.

Day #10

Traffic

Now that you have an item listed on eBay, it is time to focus on driving traffic to your auction. Getting lots of qualified traffic to see your item is a critical part of success. If you're doing everything else right, but you are having a hard time getting sales, then one of the following issues is occurring:

- You aren't getting enough people to see your product.
- Your market research is wrong, and the product is not as popular as you thought.
- Your approach to the product is not appealing.
- Your product photography is weak.
- Your copywriting is weak.

Because we have the privilege of working with so many partners, we see lots of people succeed, but sadly, we also see lots of people fail. Usually when someone fails, it is for a very obvious reason. Sadly, sometimes they email us and express frustration or say, "I just don't understand what I'm doing wrong."

Sometimes they ask us for our advice and we can tell them something like, "Work on your photography; it's not up to par." But other times people never ask. However, the most common problem people have is a lack of qualified traffic.

We list our auction items on eBay because it can generate more traffic than any other auction site. It is still the biggest and best when it comes to auction traffic. How much traffic does eBay provide and is it worth the high fees they charge?

It helps to understand how much a viewer is worth. Let's figure that out together.

If you go to an online advertising site like Google AdWords and choose to advertise for the phrase 'American Girl Doll Clothes,' you'll be told that each click you receive will cost you about 25 cents. So to get 100 clicks to your website, you'd need to spend about $25. You use this concept for your product to determine what an average visitor to your auction might be worth.

If you list an item on eBay and let it run for a standard seven-day auction, then you'll probably get around 75-150 views. So for the price of the eBay listing fee, final value fee, and every other fee that eBay charges you, they are providing you with about $25 worth of traffic.

Recently, we sold an item for $150 and the total fees were roughly $8. So if we assume eBay sent us 100 visitors, then each visitor they sent cost us eight cents. It is important to remember these aren't just any random visitors; they are qualified prospects that are looking for your type of item.

We've found only four ways to get targeted traffic less expensively than eight cents per visitor. They are:

1. Email marketing, which requires you to do newsletters.
2. YouTube, which requires you to make videos.
3. Facebook, which requires an active social media strategy.
4. Pinterest, which is one of the best possible sources of referral traffic.

In the next few chapters, we'll tackle several of these topics in a more in-depth way, but for now, let's focus on the main concept: getting more traffic and what it can mean for your business.

When we started on eBay in 2008, we would regularly have our auctions end with 100 visitors having viewed the auction. Those auctions frequently ended in the $30 to $50 range. By 2010, it was common for 250 people to view one of our auctions and sales were regularly in the $70 to $80 range. In 2011, we regularly had 500 viewers for each auction and sales were in the $100 range. In 2012, we averaged 2,000 viewers for each auction and our prices commonly exceeded $150 and went as high as $335.

When you can deliver 2,000 targeted prospects to one of your auctions in addition to the traffic that EBay sends to it, you're probably going to have a very good result. It is a numbers game.

How do we get this much qualified traffic to our auctions? We focus on the following marketing strategies:

Email Marketing: We began collecting email addresses from the very beginning — first through the eBay store function, then via an email provider. By the fall of 2009, we had collected 150 email addresses. Today we have over 21,000 email addresses. Email is the best way to get targeted traffic to your auctions. We'll explain all our tricks and strategies for email marketing on Day #12.

YouTube: We began having design contests through YouTube from the very beginning. Today we have over 8,500 subscribers and over 1.5 million video views. If you love being on camera and are interested in making videos in the how-to genre, this is an excellent way to get tons of qualified traffic. But if being on camera stresses you out, don't worry about using YouTube.

Facebook: We started our Facebook fan page in 2009 and now have over 22,000 fans. Although we generate a nice amount of traffic from Facebook, it has become less productive and more labor intensive in the last few years. But it still has its place. The biggest benefit of Facebook is that you can share a specific link, such as to your auction, and generate clicks directly to it almost immediately. That is powerful.

Pinterest: We started our Pinterest profile in December of 2011 and it has become our top source of social traffic. It delivers almost five times as much traffic to our site than Facebook does. When you consider that we only have 4,300 Pinterest followers compared to 22,000 Facebook followers, you realize how powerful Pinterest is at driving traffic. Our book _Pinterest Power_ outlines all our strategies for using Pinterest. You can get a copy on Amazon if you're interested in learning how to utilize Pinterest as a highly effective marketing tool.

A good list of prospective customers makes selling become easier, auction prices go higher, Etsy items sell faster, and new projects get a warmer welcome.

So what's the best type of traffic-generating strategy? Each type has its own strengths and weaknesses, but if we had to prioritize them we'd suggest the following top two:

Email Marketing: An email list delivers virtually free traffic. You can send an email and generate traffic any time you want it, day or night. You can write an email as often as you want. Some of the most successful email marketers send an email to people on their list every day. How can they do this? They send very helpful content, such as coupon alerts. Most importantly, an email list is a permanent part of your business assets. Facebook can shut down, Pinterest could go out of business, Twitter could ban you from their site, but an email list is your property. No one can take that away from you.

Pinterest: The traffic coming out of Pinterest is truly mind-blowing. In September of 2012, Pinterest surpassed the Yahoo! Network to become the fourth largest source of traffic on the Internet. The top sources of traffic now include:

1. Google organic search
2. direct typing of a domain name into a URL
3. Facebook
4. Pinterest

But it should be pointed out that Facebook currently has over a billion users, and Pinterest has in the range of 30 million. In another few years, Pinterest will drive more referral traffic than Facebook, making it the best website for generating referral traffic.

Here is the good news: if you worked to improve your product photography on Day #7, then you're going to have a lot of referral traffic from Pinterest. If you create a Pinterest profile and start to pin items that will appeal to your customers, then you're going to have even more traffic.

Chapter Ten Q&A with Cinnamon

Jason: How much of your success with auctions do you think is simply a result of more people seeing the auctions?

Cinnamon: It's tricky. We are definitely getting more exposure from all the new people. But when you look at who is actually winning the items, it's names of people that have been winning since the beginning. I sell items to the same people really frequently — they seem to be willing to do what it takes to get the item.

Jason: Is the fact that Pinterest is driving 10 times more traffic than your Facebook fan page good news or bad news?

Cinnamon: Well, Pinterest is amazing for new exposure. Tons of new people are finding us without having to actually do very much on that site. Our Facebook fans are more familiar with us. So when we list an auction or put up a new pattern, we can share it on Facebook and actually get more direct sales immediately because they are existing customers. So, Pinterest is good for one part of the traffic and Facebook is good for another part.

Jason: Email marketing seems like a lot of work. Is it worth it in your view?

Cinnamon: Now that I have another team member helping me with the newsletter, it is much easier to think about. You can definitely see the spikes in both traffic and sales when you send out a newsletter. People check their email more frequently and systematically than they check things on Facebook. So mentioning something on Facebook is hit-and-miss. Sometimes people see it, sometimes they don't. Sharing something in a newsletter gets a much more targeted response. In your email inbox, the message just sits there until you open it.

Jason: Is there value in advertising and buying traffic through Facebook and Google AdWords?

Cinnamon: Yes. We've done the math and can tell that the new visitors we get from these sources end up buying enough to justify paying for their visits. On Facebook, it's especially nice because we pay for them to find out about us, then they are immediately asked to join our email newsletter list. So we have a great opportunity to stay connected with them for the long-term.

Day #10 Action Step: Make a list of your current sources of potential traffic. Do you already have a Facebook profile, Twitter account, or Pinterest profile? Next, think about how you can let the people you're connected to on those platforms know about your new business venture or auction. Send out a message asking for their support. Even if they aren't your ideal customers, they are likely to support your venture because they like you.

Day #11

Home Base

Websites used to be hard to build, difficult to manage, and expensive to complete. Those days are gone. Today, a website like CraftBusinessPower.com can be set up in minutes. In fact, it *was* set up in minutes. There is no barrier to having a very nice website. If you make the commitment to achieving that goal today, you can get it done.

The total cost to set up CraftBusinessPower.com was $22.99. On the first day, the website received 341 visitors, and on the second day, 1,189 people visited the site. But if you need to spend even less than $22.99, keep reading: I'll show you how to get a good website set up for free. Or if you don't want to do any work to make that happen, I'll show you how to get one set up for as little as five bucks.

You might be wondering, *Do I really need a website?* The truth is, you can build a real business online without having a website, but you leave yourself open to a few very serious risks. So the wisest strategy for long-term success is to build a website as your home base that you can use to grow your business. Let me describe the risks of not having your own home base, and then we can walk through the setup process.

When eBay was in its prime, lots of people found a new way to make ongoing money by setting up shop on the site. Almost overnight, thousands of work-from-home entrepreneurs discovered they could make a solid income. Another breakthrough, eBay Stores, allowed users to have a storefront right on eBay. It all seemed great, but two problematic things started to happen.

The first problem was that people started to say, "I found it on eBay," not "I found it on the Dakota Mechanic Studios eBay store." To the wise brand manager, this curious omission underscored a very troubling phenomenon. I call it the 'The Platform As Provider Effect.' See, on eBay and Etsy, your brand is demoted in the mind of the customer, and the platform's brand is elevated. If you ask someone, "Hey, where'd you get that cool watch," they say "eBay." This effect must be overcome if you're going to build a thriving craft business. You must stand alone in the mind of the customer.

The second risk became clear to many eBay users when eBay started to raise its fees and focus on working with larger sellers. In the mind of many faithful users, their craft businesses were being squeezed out. And then it hit them: they had no way to communicate with their customers except via eBay, no way to keep their loyal fans as they migrated to a new site. They had relied solely on the eBay marketing machine to serve up happy customers, as needed, without an alternative form of staying connected. Of course, eBay forbade outside-eBay contact with customers, so if users obeyed their rules and wanted to leave, they were severing ties with all those eBay customers. Entrepreneurs realized at that moment that those customers were never *their* customers; they were eBay's customers.

These risks aren't confined to just eBay. It is a valid concern for any platform that serves as an intermediary between you and your customers. On August 4th, 2011, we discovered that Facebook could be just as challenging to work with. That day it shut down our account, even though we had worked for over four years to build a fan page with over 10,000 fans. In an instant, all that was 'closed.' Luckily, we were able to appeal that decision and our fan page was reactivated, but not before we learned a valuable lesson. You cannot let a third-party website have control over your customer relationships. You must maintain the ability to stay in direct contact with your customers. The only way to do that is by having your own website and your own email list. Fortunately, you can set up both for free.

Let's look at how website creation can be done most easily based on a few different scenarios:

Zero dollars to spend and you're willing to do a bit of work. If you literally cannot spend even $5 to get a website set up, then your best approach is to use a WordPress.com website. Simply visit WordPress.com and follow their simple instructions. They provide you with a free website, and it is very simple to set up. The catch is that you will not be able to use a completely unique domain name. For the privilege of using their system for free, they require you to have a domain that includes the '.wordpress.com' ending. So if your new company name is Crafter's Business Power, your domain name would be www.craftersbusinesspower.wordpress.com. That's not so bad, for free. An alternative to WordPress is Moonfruit.com. It provides a nice collection of tools, with both free and paid options. While I haven't used it, I've heard very positive reviews.

Five dollars to spend and you're not willing to do any work. If you want someone else to set up a WordPress site for you, simply visit Fiverr.com and look for the gigs on this topic. People will do an amazing amount of work for you, all for five bucks. Of course, you're going to need to learn how to add content to your new blog, so in some ways, even if you don't want to do the setup yourself, it's probably a good learning experience.

Twenty-three dollars to spend and you're willing to do a bit of work. If you're willing to spend the money, you can purchase a unique domain name from GoDaddy.com and have your WordPress site linked to it for another $13, which you pay to WordPress.com. So for just under $23, you can have a WordPress.com website with a unique domain that indicates to the world that you are a bit more professional than an entry-level WordPress user.

Twenty-eight dollars to spend and you're not willing to do any work. As you might guess, if you're willing to pay for someone on Fiverr to do it, they'll set up your new WordPress site and also link up your unique domain. As with the prior Fiverr option, you'll still need to learn how to add content to your blog, so setting it up yourself might be a good learning experience.

The good news is that each of these providers — GoDaddy, WordPress, and Fiverr — all have video tutorials, help desks, and resource guides that will assist you and walk you through how to do these things. Additionally, if you search on YouTube, you can find tutorials to instruct you on each step in the process.

If you decide you want to really jump into the deep end of the pool and set up a fully functional e-commerce site from the very beginning, then there is one site I'd recommend: Shopify.com. If you're willing to pay $29 a month and want a very good e-commerce solution that will allow you to sell items, build a customer list, and list up to 100 items, Shopify is for you. But if that seems like too big of a step, don't worry. You can always grow into it when the timing is right.

Chapter Eleven Q&A with Cinnamon

Jason: What are you thoughts on setting up websites?

Cinnamon: They are easy to set up, but you shouldn't underestimate the amount of time they can take to keep updated. They're a lot of work, but totally worth it. You need to have a website. You should definitely start with a great name, then see if it is available at GoDaddy.com, then have the logo created, then apply it to your various websites.

Jason: What else do you think people might be confused about?

Cinnamon: Well, people don't understand that a blog is a website. There is really no difference these days. People also need to decide how they are going to use various sites, and be clear about what each site is used for. Sometimes Facebook is the right place to do something, sometimes your website is, sometimes your eBay or Etsy store is.

Jason: What have you done to integrate your websites into social media locations?

Cinnamon: You definitely want a consistent look and feel as much as possible. Each site is different, but you can always use your logo or other visual elements. Plus, you should always be consistent with the written description of who you are and what you do. Getting a logo made in several file formats, and in a way that can work in multiple types of situations, is really important.

Jason: Where would you recommend people start if they want a logo, but are just beginning to get this whole process figured out?

Cinnamon: There are packages on Etsy where people will make a custom logo that will fit in various spaces. You can also find people on Fiverr.com that will make custom logos or custom Facebook fan page images. You can also go to PicMonkey.com, which has templates you can use to create various Facebook elements. It all starts with a great logo, and then you can apply it to the various sites.

Jason: What do you do when something goes wrong with a website?

Cinnamon: I think the main thing to remember is that the companies you're using all have help services and are there to help you. Some are better than others, but usually if you need help they have a way to support you. So don't be afraid to ask. Always make sure you have the support phone numbers or contact method saved somewhere. I have our hosting account phone number saved in my phone contacts. So when there is a problem, I immediately hit them on the speed dial and they help get it fixed.

Day #11 Action Step: Decide on a budget for your website and the most appropriate path for your situation. Jump into your chosen solution and struggle through the learning curve. Make a goal to have your website finished as quickly as possible. If you use Fiverr, it might take a few days, unless you pay extra to have it done within 24 hours.

Day #12

You've Got Mail

When we started selling on eBay, we made the decision to open an eBay Store. One of the features of those stores is the ability to collect email addresses and send out newsletters to the subscribers. So from the very beginning, we got in the habit of collecting email addresses and sending out a newsletter on Saturday or Sunday before our auctions would end. Our customary routine was to list our auctions so they'd end at 6:00 PM Pacific on Sunday night. The email would go out earlier on Sunday so that when people opened it, they could immediately go onto eBay and see the current price of our auction items. If they were interested, they could jump into the bidding.

By the fall of 2009, we had 150 names on our email list. We realized that if we could grow that list faster, we could potentially drive a lot more traffic to our auctions. So we moved our email marketing out of the eBay system and learned to do it on our own. We began adding a few hundred names to our email list per month. By 2011, we had learned new skills and started adding a hundred names a week. Now we are adding roughly 300-500 new names to our email list per week, or close to 1,500 to 1,800 per month. We now have over 21,000 names on our list, and by the time you read this, that number will be much higher.

An email list is one of the most important marketing tools you can create. Why is it so valuable? Consider the following reasons:

1. An email list is something that you own and control completely. That means it is a long-term business asset. If you build a list of 100,000 email addresses made up of people interested in the craft niche, you will have a very valuable craft business.

2. An email list is not tied to your Etsy, eBay, or Facebook account. Even if people originally connect with you on those platforms, when they join your email list, they become your prospects. If Facebook shuts down your account or goes out of business, you still have the relationships with the people who have joined your email list.

3. An email list allows you to control your traffic, or at least strongly influence it. Want visitors on Sunday afternoon? No problem.

4. Email marketing allows you to build rapport with a large number of people and

become a 'trusted resource.'

5. You can segment your list and develop new lists of people interested in different topics. To finish this book, *Craft Business Power*, we sent several messages to several different lists. We asked them to help us review this book, and to do that they had to join a new list. That new list immediately received 375 people who agreed to help us and we had a group of people whom we could work with on a new topic — the *Craft Business Power* book project.

Direct Marketing News did an extensive survey and found that when it comes to opening newsletters and marketing emails, people have an inner circle of 16 trusted senders on average. In other words, people will immediately open an email from approximately 16 marketers or companies — people they know, like, and trust. Beyond that, people have a filter that kicks in that allows them to begin screening unwanted messages. They will possibly open an email from people outside this trusted 16 based on the subject line, time of year, amount of time available, or any of dozens of other factors.

So how do you build a vibrant email list? The best way is called the Organic Model. The way the model works is fairly simple. It has two primary parts.

First, you offer a free newsletter which people

must sign up to receive by providing their email address. The free email newsletter is commonly sent weekly, bimonthly, or monthly. It can also be a daily email, if that makes sense for your purposes. For example, 'Sign Up for Our Daily Inspirational Quote' or 'Sign Up for Our Weekly Newsletter.' The main thing is that you label it clearly from the beginning so that people know what they are signing up for.

Second, you need to find an ever-growing list of places to mention or advertise your free newsletter. These might include:

- your eBay 'About Me' page
- your Facebook fan page
- your website
- your email footer
- your packaging materials that you mail to customers with their purchases
- your blog
- editorial mentions or interviews

The list of possible locations to advertise your free newsletter is endless, as long as you comply with the Terms of Service of the online location where you're advertising it. Many times, these sources take some time and energy to set up, but once established they can continue to provide new sign-ups for a very long time. Your advertisement doesn't point people to your homepage or product; it points people to a page to sign up for your newsletter.

Once people discover your email newsletter and sign up, they become part of your email list. Many marketers simply refer to this as their 'list' or 'house list.' Once you have people on your list, you can begin emailing them. You must honor the intention of the subscribers, so you cannot spam them with unrelated emails. But when done wisely, you can weave many topics into your newsletters that will be accepted by your readers.

How did we go from 150 email addresses to 21,000 in three years? We did it with a very simple strategy as part of the launch of our pattern business. We offered two free patterns as an incentive. This is not an original idea; it is a very common marketing strategy. Some people call it an ethical bribe.

The most common way to boost the number of people willing to sign up to receive your email newsletter is by offering them a nice gift as an incentive. This can be a how-to guide, a special report, a webinar or video, or in our case, two free patterns. When we started offering our incentives, the number of people signing up for our newsletter went from a few people per week to over 100 per week. The results were shocking. We will look into this further in the next chapter.

I hope we've convinced you that email marketing is a very wise investment of your time and energy. Now let's talk about how to build a solid list of subscribers using completely free tools.

Six Steps to Building an Effective Email
Newsletter System:

Find an email management system. Your
first step is to find an email management system
that you like. There are lots of options. We
consistently use two different providers. One is
MailChimp. It allows you to use the service for
free until you have over 2,000 people on your
email list. It's a great deal for people just starting
out. We also use Constant Contact, which is
another good option, but is not as generous for
beginners. Constant Contact is not free past 60
days of use. These email management systems
will store names, provide templates, and allow
people to unsubscribe, which is a legal
requirement.

Learn to use the system. Email marketing
systems all operate in slightly different ways.
Most have a resource center and even guides to
walk you through the process. You'll want to learn
about best practices as well as the legal aspects of
emailing people. If you decide to use MailChimp,
then you'll be excited to know they have resources
for lots of different topics. They even have an e-
book for online sellers and another for designers.

Set up your welcome email. The welcome
email is the one a new subscriber will receive
when they are added to your list. In addition to
being a very friendly thank-you, it can also
explain more about your business and most
importantly, it is the place to deliver your gift or

incentive. In our case, for our weekly newsletter incentive of two free patterns, we provide a link in the welcome email to an online location where the two free patterns can be downloaded.

Set up your orientation sequence. All email marketing systems have what is called an 'auto-responder system.' It is a set of pre-written emails that go out automatically to people who sign up for your email list. You write these messages one time and they are sent out to each new person that signs up. These messages go out on top of any newsletters you might produce. You can use these to educate and orient your new list subscribers. For subscribers of the Liberty Jane Clothing newsletter, we mention in the welcome email that they will get a series of 'special messages' from Cinnamon over the next few days. We tell them that these will provide everything they need to know about Liberty Jane Clothing. These messages serve several purposes:

1. They help bond the new subscriber to us.

2. They help explain all the ways a new subscriber can participate in your business. Some examples might be where you blog, the name of your Twitter or Facebook fan page, when you run sales or promotions, when you list your items, or your approach to your craft and how it is different.

3. They act as a filter. If people aren't serious about Liberty Jane Clothing, then by the

end of day three or four, they will likely unsubscribe because they've grown tired of receiving these daily messages. That's fine. We'd rather have people who are really interested added to our list.

4. They serve as a way to convert prospects into buyers. In our welcome sequence, on the last 'special message' we provide a 'special offer.' It is a discount to try out our products. We consider this our conversion step. We want to convert them from being a freebie seeker to being a real customer.

Determine the type of newsletter you're going to send out. Most email service providers including MailChimp have templates you can use to make very nice email newsletters. Another option is to make a simpler, plain text newsletter. The choice is up to you. When you're trying to sell physical or digital products, having pictures is probably a key part of the newsletter. But when you are simply providing announcements or information, a plain text email is probably fine. Once you establish a style, you can become more efficient at producing the newsletter and your readers will become accustomed to it.

Integrate your sign-up form. Once you've established an email marketing account and have created a list that people can subscribe to, you need to integrate the sign-up form into your website. If you followed the website directions on Day #11 and decided that a free WordPress account is for you, then you can find many online tutorials and guides for integrating your email sign-up form into your WordPress site. If you're stuck, then simply go to Fiverr.com and pay someone $5 to install the code for you.

Chapter Twelve Q&A with Cinnamon

Jason: What are you thoughts about email marketing?

Cinnamon: This is definitely a part of the business that is guided by you more than me, although I can definitely see its importance.

Jason: What is the hardest part of doing an ongoing newsletter?

Cinnamon: Deciding what to talk about, especially in weeks when you don't have something new that you're selling. You definitely need to find ways to revisit topics or create interest in upcoming projects. You also have to remember that you have brand new people joining your list every week. For us, that's almost 500 a week, so it makes you realize you need to write in a way that is friendly to brand-new readers. In our category, we see American Girl do this all the time —they re-market existing products with energy and enthusiasm. You have to learn how to do that, too.

Jason: Do you feel like using images is a

requirement for a good newsletter?

Cinnamon: Most retail newsletters are image intensive. They are much more interesting when you're selling a product. When you're selling a service, the written content is probably more important than the images.

Jason: What type of incentive or ethical bribe would you encourage entrepreneurs to create if they're having a hard time with that part?

Cinnamon: If you're selling physical products, coupons are one option, but for us, they conflict with our selling philosophy. Sometimes we give coupons, but we aren't doing it aggressively. Guides or how-to e-books are always good — anything that you can create that people will see as having a high perceived value.

Jason: What's the top strategy you'd recommend for people using newsletters?

Cinnamon: Use the newsletter to drive people to your website. You don't need to fill it completely. Just include enough to get people interested and then have them click through to your website to continue reading or shopping.

Day #12 Action Step: Decide on an email provider and register for a free account. Go to the provider's resource section and begin learning about email marketing best practices. Decide on your style of newsletter and how frequently it will go out. Work through the setup steps to integrate your newsletter into your website.

Day #13

Free

Getting customers to show up and buy an item is hard work. You can use all sorts of tricks to try to make that happen, and some strategies are better than others. You've got to decide how you are going to use the power of free to benefit your business.

Many companies offer discounts out of desperation to sell items. They place their items on sale at a certain percentage off. It's the classic '50% off sale' approach. These marketers figure that people love a sale and it is better to move items, even if it is at a discount, than to not sell items at all. By offering an item for 50% off, you are in fact giving half of it away for free.

The financial damage caused by these types of discounts cannot be overestimated. Most companies exist with a small percentage of total sales that turn into net profit. The net profit is possible only if you sell your items for more than it costs you to make them. When you discount your products in order to sell them, you give away your profit.

This type of discount strategy has another problematic side effect: it is addictive. Like a bad drug that, once worn off, leaves the victim feeling more desperate for another dose, it does real damage to the psyche of business owners. They become dependent on the constant infusion of quick cash. It is not uncommon to see a company start a discounting strategy and then escalate it to a level of almost constant use.

It is also addictive for customers. They become accustomed to waiting for your coupons and discounts before they'll purchase. So while a discount boosts sales in the short-term, in the long-term it acts to suppress sales. Rather than a customer acting on their impulse to buy a new item, they think, *I should wait for the next sale or coupon.* The more frequently you run a sale or discount, the more likely customers are to have the idea of a coupon pop into their mind that stops them from making an immediate purchase. Make the decision early in your business to use coupons and discounts very rarely.

The good news is that there is another form of free that can add a lot of value and get you the results you want. Let's review three fantastic ways to use the power of free:

Contests: As a leader in your niche, you have the ability to impress people with your ability to make interesting items. Creating a fun contest that engages your customers and gives away a free custom-made item as the prize is a simple way to generate traffic and enthusiasm.

Information Products: As we discovered on Day #9, an information product is a non-rival good. Once you make a digital product like a how-to guide, the cost to give it away becomes zero. These items, when they have a high perceived value, make excellent free gifts. As we mentioned in the last chapter, we use two free patterns as the incentive to sign up for our newsletter.

Giveaways: When you are committed to resisting the discounts and coupons model, you'll find a few times during the year very tempting. The Christmas shopping season is probably the most challenging. One way to substitute a productive version of free at this time of year is to do a giveaway. For the last few years, we've done a '12 Days of Christmas' giveaway. Our customers seem to really enjoy that approach, and it seems to satisfy their need for free items.

Chapter Thirteen Q&A with Cinnamon

Jason: How did you come up with the idea to hold YouTube design contests as a giveaway strategy?

Cinnamon: We noticed that tons of girls were on YouTube making videos for each other. It created a lot of traffic. So when we started putting up our videos, they started commenting and becoming fans. We thought we'd make a contest that fit with what they were doing.

Jason: Were you afraid of having to make an outfit that someone else designed?

Cinnamon: No. I knew I could make whatever they designed, and I could pick the winner. So I'd only pick something that I knew I could do well and that would be interesting.

Jason: Did you worry giving away free patterns? Since that strategy has been so successful, looking back was it an unfounded fear?

Cinnamon: You wanted to do it initially. I didn't understand it, but now that we have hundreds of patterns, it doesn't seem to be too big of a concern.

Jason: How did you come up with the 12 Days Of Christmas giveaway?

Cinnamon: It was November and we thought, *Hey, we should do a 12 Days of Christmas giveaway*. I don't remember exactly how we thought of that, but after we did, we noticed that tons of companies do it. Now the challenge is to come up with interesting things to give away.

Jason: Are there mistakes to avoid when it comes to free?

Cinnamon: Free is fun, but it is also hard to do because of the amount of time and effort involved in making handmade items. So I'd never suggest that you give away something that you feel is too valuable in terms of time or money. But then again, my custom-made outfits for the YouTube contests are fairly time intensive.

Day #13 Action Step: Take the time to journal about your approach to free. Under what circumstances will you offer a discount or coupon? Plan now for your first year's giveaway and contest strategies. Work on an information product that you can give away to your customers. Decide what type of item you might give away as an incentive to sign up for your newsletter and customize it as needed. If you need to create it, begin that work.

Day #14

Product Launches

When you make a product and prepare to sell it, you get to decide how you are going to reveal it to the public. This is called your product launch. There are lots of options available and how you do it determines the results you'll get. The launch announcement, price, product photography, copywriting, and method of selling (either auction or fixed-price), all swirl together to create an overall impression that influences your audience. You get to decide whether to dedicate an entire newsletter to the launch, or maybe just make a casual mention of it on your Facebook page.

If done well, you have an opportunity to launch it in a way that generates enthusiasm, interest, and buzz. Correctly planned product launches are a terrific way to drive massive amounts of traffic and sell items very quickly. Well-designed product launches make it clear to your customers that buying the item quickly is wise, or they'll likely miss out.

If your product is launched poorly, then the result is fairly predictable: little or no enthusiasm, few sales, no buzz. This result is incredibly common. Good products, nicely designed and constructed, sit for far too long on Etsy. The most common reason is that the sellers don't do any type of product launch efforts. But it doesn't have to be that way. Product launches, like the other parts of an effective marketing plan, are learned skills. Once the steps are understood and mastered, they become second nature. Once they are second nature, selling becomes easy.

Let's look at two examples, then walk through the common elements in an effective product launch.

We sell a certain type of doll shoes for $21 a pair. They are a miniature version of TOMS that we call Janes. The design was an immediate hit. They are hard for us to keep in stock and our customers know it. The shoes are handmade for us in the U.S.A. in small batches of six or eight. Each time we get a batch, we list them on our website and then include an update in our next newsletter. We tell people that the shoes will quickly sell out, so if they want a pair, they should buy them quickly — and they immediately sell out. Recently, instead of placing a message about the Janes in our newsletter, we took a picture and shared it on Instagram. Again, they immediately sold out. This is a very simple product launch approach that is supported by a simple communication plan. It is enough to sell all that we have in stock.

We conduct a Design Academy several times a year. It is a month-long program and participants pay $79. They get 12 lessons taught by Cinnamon and the Liberty Jane team. It is a very fun event that the participants seem to really enjoy. People like it so much that they re-enroll and take it more than once. When we first came up with this idea and tried to launch it, we had 20 participants. That's not a bad result, but we thought we could do better. The second time we conducted it, we launched it in a similar way and had a similar number of participants. Then we took the time to learn how to do product launches for this type of unique event. The next time we conducted the course, we had 104 participants. That's over $8,000 in revenue. For this type of event, we had to learn to do the launch sequence differently than how we launch a clothing product. Once we learned how to do the launch sequence properly, the results changed dramatically.

Common Product Launch Elements:

The Sideways Sales Letter: Jeff Walker is considered the pioneer of the product launch concept and he coined the phrase the 'sideways sales letter.' The idea is that rather than having a very long online sales letter that goes on for page after page, you take the content and break it into smaller chunks. You share those chunks in a series of pre-launch messages that build up to the launch event.

The Pre-Launch Story: There is a reason you're making a new product. Think hard about that reason. Maybe customers are requesting it frequently. Maybe you developed a new concept after a trip to Europe. Maybe you really wanted the item for yourself, and now you're going to make them available to your customers. A powerful or interesting pre-launch story has the ability to emotionally engage your customers in a profound way. Pre-selling starts with capturing the interest of your prospective buyers.

Sneak-Peek Photography: The pre-launch story can be shared with a few images of the construction process. Giving people a glimpse of the new item acts as a tease. It permits you to include them in the journey toward the finished product.

The Sale Date Announcement: Rather than simply running an auction or creating an Etsy listing, you want to inform your customers that you're going to be doing it. You want them very aware of what you're doing. You should communicate in advance, as clearly as possible, when you will be launching your products.

What does a standard product launch sequence look like?

It really varies depending on the significance of the product. At Liberty Jane, we have two significant product launches related to our new designs: our Spring and Fall Line launches. But throughout the year, we are always launching something. It may be a new batch of Janes, a Design Academy course, a new e-book, a design contest, a new pattern, a giveaway, or some other product or service.

Our Spring Line and Fall Lines each feature three to five outfits. Every outfit is listed separately on eBay, one after the other, over the course of several weeks. Let's look at the steps we use to launch these auctions:

Three Weeks Prior: We dedicate a good portion of our newsletter to sharing our enthusiasm for the new line and any interesting details. We start to share the pre-launch story. We let people know when we will be launching the first auction and how many outfits we will be including in the line. We also reference how the last auctions ended from the prior line, being sure to mention the price the last auction ended at as a way to set people's expectations.

Two Weeks Prior: We include a picture of the first item in the newsletter, even if it is just an image of the fabric choices. We will mention the specific launch date and time. Sometimes we share a picture of Cinnamon shopping for fabric, or a picture of the inspiration outfit she used to come up with the design.

One Week Prior: We share more details about the story of the first outfit and the photos. We also share more details about the second or third outfit in the line.

Auction Launch Day: We generally publish our

newsletters on a Saturday or Sunday, so we try to time it so the auction goes live and we have a link to our eBay store or directly to the auction listing. That newsletter is focused on announcing the launch. We always run our auctions for seven days, ending on a Sunday night around 6:00 PM Pacific.

Seven Days Later: We place a reminder about the auction on our Facebook fan page several hours before the auction ends. We also try to send out our newsletter so that it arrives in people's email inboxes a few hours before the end of the auction. In the newsletter, we have a link to the auction so that even if people read the newsletter after the auction has ended, they can click through and see how high the final bid price finished. This newsletter will also announce the second outfit in our launch with a link to that auction. That second auction begins right when the first auction ends and runs for seven days.

Another Seven Days Later: We repeat this cycle for several weeks as the auctions are underway. Our newsletters might mention other items, but the primary focus is the auctions that are occurring.

The beauty of a Spring and Fall Line is that your customers grow accustomed to the process. They begin to anticipate it happening and grow excited even before you announce it. After the auctions end, we take a screenshot of the final bid price and place it on our blog, reinforcing to our customers the prices we obtained for the outfits.

As we were writing this e-book, we finished the Fall 2012 auctions. We auctioned four outfits. The final bid prices were as follows: $86, $197, $127, and $272. It is not uncommon for us to have our first auction end at the lowest price and our last auction end at the highest price. Many bidders participate, but don't win, and over the course of the four weeks, they become more desperate to win. We have used this same auction launch strategy for five years with very consistent results.

Each product is different, and each product launch you do will be different. Launching a batch of new Janes is different from an auction. Your job is to experiment and discover the sequence of steps that are optimal for creating enthusiasm, customer interest, and ultimately sales. Selling becomes easy when you master the product launch formula.

Chapter Fourteen Q&A with Cinnamon:

Jason: How do you feel about the Product Launch model?

Cinnamon: I think if you're selling a physical product, then product launches are a great idea. It gives people a reason to support your work. If you do it systematically, people know what to expect and that helps a lot.

Jason: Do you think sending information before the auction, during it, and right at the end is too much communication?

Cinnamon: Well, that's why I like to have my auctions start and end right at the same time so you can bundle the messages. I think if it was one single auction, then three messages would be too much.

Jason: How do you use newsletters and social media together to help launch products?

Cinnamon: It's nice to have different tools so that you can alternate or bounce around from one type of communication to another so people don't feel like you're overdoing it. So including launch details in the newsletter, then next time just via Facebook or Pinterest, is a good approach.

Jason: How did promoting your Janes shoes on Instagram work?

Cinnamon: It was pretty easy. Our designer was finishing up a batch of cute red Janes and she sent me a picture to show me what she had finished and was about to put in the mail. I simply shared it on Instagram and said, "Red Janes are on their way." The response was very enthusiastic and people really liked seeing in advance what was going to happen. A week later, I listed them and they sold out immediately. There were six pairs at $21 apiece.

Jason: What's your biggest challenge with product launches?

Cinnamon: Being totally behind and wanting to cancel the whole thing. But when you announce a launch date and people are expecting it, you're stuck.

Jason: If someone is used to simply listing things on Etsy without any launch strategy, what would be a good first step?

Cinnamon: I don't know; I would ask them! It seems like a mistake to have items in your Etsy shop that sit there longer than a week, so I'd work to come up with a plan. When people have stuff that just sit in their stores, it makes it seem like it's something nobody wants. You've got to come up with ways to not let that happen.

Day #14 Action Step: Take one product and write down a series of launch steps for it. Consider ways you can break up information in a way that gets people excited. Develop a compelling launch story and decide how to share it. Even if you only have a handful of email addresses or a very small following on Facebook, begin to develop the discipline of launching new products in a robust way.

Day #15

Help

The choices you make related to adding people to your team can be painfully difficult. This will challenge you to the very core of who you are. You can refuse to add any help and control everything, but that will radically limit your success. You can add help to assist you in an area that you are weak in, or add help to assist you in an area that you are strong in. If you want a profitable craft business that is more than just a job, you really need to think deeply about how to tackle this tough issue.

According to finance author and educator Robert Kiyosaki, there are five core business concepts that must be well managed. Most of the time, a crafter starting out in business will be focused on just one of the core aspects — the product — but that is not enough. Let's review the five core aspects:

Product: The product creation effort is the most tangible part of a business. A great product can make a great company, but not if the other parts of the business aren't put together properly. As Cinnamon described in the Introduction, our business grew out of her ability to make contemporary doll clothes.

Legal: The legal structure of the business is the formal foundation upon which you build. There are several choices related to how to incorporate. How and when you take these steps is critical to your success. It is a serious mistake to ignore this aspect of your new craft business. Getting the help of a good tax advisor or CPA is the simplest way to ensure you're off to a great start. In addition to articles of incorporation, there are legal issues related to local business licensing, state and federal tax requirements, and compliance with other federal, state, and local ordinances.

Systems: When you use Etsy or eBay, you are using their selling system. A business is a system made up of smaller systems. Several of the chapters in this book are descriptions of selling systems or advertising systems. The more you master specific systems, the stronger your business will grow. At Liberty Jane Clothing, both Cinnamon and I have a primary business focus: hers is product and mine is communications, but we both share a secondary focus on systems. When our website goes down, neither of us hesitate to pick up the phone and call our hosting company to get it resolved.

Marketing/Communications: This book has largely been focused on this one business discipline, which includes branding, sales, social media, copywriting, photography, and every other aspect of the public presentation of the company. Over the last five years, as we've worked to build Liberty Jane Clothing, we've encountered literally hundreds of crafters who make extraordinary products, but who don't have help in the marketing department. That is why we established Liberty Jane Partners, The Cutting Room, and even why we wrote this book. Show me a great entrepreneur and I'll show you someone who has learned to be great at selling their products.

Cash Flow: Managing the revenue and expenses of your business is vital to your success. Somebody has to learn to be a good bookkeeper. When we started Liberty Jane Clothing, we had a financial goal in mind, but we knew we needed to spend money to build the business. We considered it our investment into the startup effort. On some occasions, we needed things and made a personal investment into the business by using our own money to make the purchase. Sometimes we waited until we sold products to buy needed business items. Sometimes we used a credit card and paid it off later, although we would not advise doing that very often. Eventually, we made promises to pay people in the future in anticipation of having the necessary money. That is how both payroll and royalty payments tend to operate. This isn't wrong; it's just a function of forecasting your income. Effectively managing your new craft business's revenue and expenses is a skill you must master. There is only one thing worse than not making any sales — it is working like crazy to make a lot of sales, but then realizing you did not making any profit because your expenses equaled or exceeded sales. Good cash flow management turns sales into profits.

This list of business duties can seem overwhelming. Most business owners are good in one area. Sometimes a business owner gets lucky and is good in multiple areas. At Liberty Jane, we got lucky because as co-founders, we were good in two different areas and fairly good at a third. If you want to grow a profitable craft business, you'll need to decide what you're good at and what you're not good at, and work to creatively fill in the gaps. Ultimately, you'll need to decide what you most enjoy and hire people in other areas so that you can work in the part of the business that you love. As the owner, it is your job to make sure that each of the five core duties is professionally handled.

Each craft business will be different because each founder's skill-set is different. You might be wondering how we have tackled these issues over the last five years as we've grown Liberty Jane. While we are not suggesting that this is a playbook for your success because your situation will be unique, we thought you might like to see how we have grown. Here is the list of people we have added to our team, in order of appearance. Some of these people are service providers that we use in an ongoing way, some have become employees, and some were just used one time to accomplish a project.

<u>Year One:</u>

CPA: Our Certified Public Accountant originally helped us file our taxes properly as a Sole Proprietorship the first year. Later, he helped us set up a Limited Liability Corporation (LLC) and understand how to do the basic accounting to ensure we were handling our expenses properly. Eventually, our CPA began helping us manage our payroll and other state and federal compliance issues. This is an ongoing relationship that is critical to our success.

eBay Store Designer: Our eBay store design and corporate logo were both done by a designer in London. It was a one-time relationship that cost us $250. It helped us set up our original store through eBay the way we wanted.

<u>Year Two:</u>

Website Expert: We feel incredibly blessed to have found a very good website expert early on. Shirley is based in New York and uses a team of technical wizards based largely in India. Her work is fast, friendly, and cheap. We are frequently amazed at the amount of work that her team will do for $200. Additionally, Shirley has helped us learn a tremendous amount about websites, Internet issues, and related concepts. By learning to sell products directly on our own websites, we reduce our dependency on sites like eBay and

Etsy, although we still use them.

Year Three:

House Cleaner: Three years later, we were ready to add help to make our business more productive. But the added cost was actually part of our personal expenses. What position did we add? We had someone start cleaning our house regularly. This allowed us to spend more time on the business.

Master Seamstress: We also added a master seamstress to the team that year. Dawne Ester works with us long distance from the East Coast. She helps complete our buy-it-now items. Her work is extraordinary; she is a true master seamstress. She helps us keep items in stock as much as we can.

Social Media Coordinator: In year three, Facebook and other customer communication efforts were taking up a lot of Cinnamon's time, leaving little time for product creation. So we added a social media person who helped us keep our Facebook efforts alive. When that person decided to move on, we expanded the role to a customer service position and hired Cammie Reagan. Now she handles most of the customer service, social media, and newsletter-related responsibilities.

Intellectual Property Attorney: We also began a relationship with a premiere intellectual property attorney in Seattle. This person earns an impressive amount of money each time we visit his office. Going to the 48th floor of the Columbia Tower in downtown Seattle is always an amazing journey. We consider this a cost of doing business. You may never need to work with an attorney of this type, but in our case, it became a necessity.

Business Advisors: In year three, we also met with three very influential people. While we did not employ them, we did consider them significant to the business, so I thought I would list them here. One was a professor of Fashion Industry at Seattle Pacific University. Jaeil Lee has a Ph.D. in Fashion Industry and was a former designer at Abercrombie & Fitch. She was incredibly encouraging and helped us envision how we might grow bigger. We also met the founder of Ex-Officio, one of Seattle's most iconic clothing brands. His advice was very helpful as well. He was tremendously gracious and encouraging, and our work with him was a highlight of the year. He explained how he went from startup, to fast-paced growth, to ultimately selling his company. Finally, through our church we've become good friends with a local business owner. He owns and runs Dairy Queen franchises. Although he works in a completely different industry, his real-world experience has been extremely helpful. He helped us improve our bookkeeping, how to think about transaction costs, and how to deal with payroll-related issues. You'd be amazed at how helpful successful business owners are willing to be.

<u>Year Four:</u>

Designers: In our fourth year, we added two incredibly talented designers to the team. First, we hired Karin Pascho. Karin came to us after 13 years at Nordstrom Product Group as a Senior Designer. When you walk through the mall with Karin and people walk past you, she can point out garments that she has personally designed. That blows our minds. We are incredibly blessed to work with her and consider her an absolute master at design, clothing construction, and pattern making. She has an extensive technical design background and she has elevated the quality and professionalism of our work. We were also thrilled to have Melinda Schlimmer join us. Melinda is the design genius behind the Melody Valerie Couture doll clothing line. Her intensity of detail and ability to make incredibly intricate garments is absolutely fascinating to watch. She is a master doll clothes maker.

Shoe Maker: In the fourth year, we also added Bee Jacobs to the team to help us keep up with the customer demand for our popular Janes shoes. Bee is truly gifted at constructing these cute little shoes, which is not as easy as it might sound. Similarly to Dawne Ester, our master seamstress, we pay Bee per piece.

Literary Agent: We also began a relationship with an amazing agent in New York. She found us through the *Pinterest Power* book project. Since then, she's helped us secure two more social media book contracts, as well as a sewing-related book contract. The large publishers are all based in New York, and Marilyn has amazing connections in the publishing industry. Her insight and wisdom are an incredible blessing. Marilyn works on commission and is paid from the proceeds of advance and royalty payments from publishing companies we work with.

As we move into our fifth year in business, we will definitely be adding more people to our team. What you need to add next is always a hard choice to make. Sometimes you know you need to add help to resolve an issue, but you're not sure of the best way to get the job done. Here is how we look at adding people to the team:

Helpers: Helpers take over something that you are currently doing that you want to delegate. Frequently, these people are paid by the hour and are considered employees. Sometimes they can be considered independent contractors. If you can add someone to do the simpler activities, especially the ones that you dislike doing, then your time can be freed up to do more productive things. Helpers can be entry-level positions or senior level positions. I am a co-founder and work on the marketing efforts, but I consider myself a helper, making sure the marketing work gets done so that Cinnamon can do the design work that she loves.

Professional Service Providers: Working with a service provider can sometimes be a one-time event, or it can be an ongoing relationship. Many times, it is wise to pay someone for their expertise, especially in technical and legal areas like accounting or law. Other examples are website experts, literary agents, or one-time consultants that help you solve a specific issue. Then there are companies that provide a product that you need to grow your business. Etsy, eBay, and PayPal all fall into this category.

Production Team Members: You might wonder why we hired two incredibly gifted designers when that is one of Cinnamon's areas of strength. The answer is simple. Adding technical design talent to the team provided us with the ability to go even deeper into the area of our strength. We want to have the most talented design team any doll clothes company has ever seen. The heart of our business is design, and everything else is built to support that part. Our product people also include the seamstresses and shoe makers that make the product a reality.

There is a final category of help that you need to consider, and that is cooperative help from other sellers in your niche. Many people in the doll clothes niche expected us to be competitive because, in their view, we were competing against the other sellers. But that is never how we looked at it. We have always believed that as small sellers in our niche, we are stronger working together than we are working alone.

The beautiful part of a craft business is that you can start small, dream big, and build the company you want. There are thousands of people waiting to help you grow. It is not easy deciding how to add help, but if you can do it effectively, your craft business will grow.

Chapter Fifteen Q&A with Cinnamon:

Jason: What's the hardest part about having people help you?

Cinnamon: I'm a control freak. So taking the time to teach someone what you do is hard. Knowing that you've found the right person is hard. Trusting that people can actually do something and be good at it is hard. It takes time for people to learn your business.

Jason: Would you rather add people to cover your areas of weakness or add people to improve upon your strengths?

Cinnamon: Well, currently I spend too much time on computer-related issues, like our websites. So I definitely need to improve that part of our operation.

Jason: What's been the best part of adding help?

Cinnamon: It's nice to have other people working on your projects. You turn around and things are done. The pressure is off of me. There is definitely an energy that comes with working with other people, too. It helps me be excited about working on something new.

Jason: What has it meant to get input from professional advisors, people like Jaeil Lee?

Cinnamon: Meeting with Jaeil was really exciting. I didn't expect her to have any interest in what I was doing. I didn't expect her to think it was a real part of the fashion design world. She was genuinely impressed and excited about our efforts. It was very flattering. Hearing her describe how design work happened at Abercrombie & Fitch was fun, too.

Jason: Any final thoughts on asking for help?

Cinnamon: Asking for help is hard for me, but it's the right thing to do and has been very rewarding. I realize it can be hard for people who are perfectionists, but when you find the right people for the right job, it is truly great.

Day Fifteen Action Step: In your journal, write down your reflections on the five core aspects of a business: Product, Legal, Systems, Marketing, and Cash Flow. Outline your approach to each one to determine what gaps might exist. Pencil in the names of people who you think have expertise in one of the areas that you consider a gap. Think about how and when to approach them for advice.

Conclusion

When it comes to growing a craft business, the first 15 days are just the start. We hope these lessons have helped shape your thinking about how to structure your business.

Of course, there are more lessons that when learned well swirl together to create a thriving small business. Some lessons can be learned in a day and immediately add value to your business. Other lessons are more difficult to accept or understand.

The really hard lessons frequently involve the entrepreneur overcoming mental or emotional resistance to an idea. These can take years to learn. Regardless of whether they come quickly or slowly, the entrepreneur's job is to find and implement new lessons that enable revenue growth.

In our first year in business, we sold $12,000 in product, which felt like a good start for us. We had to learn how to modify our business process and strategies to grow beyond that point. We had to learn how to build our brand.

In our second year, we started to make changes, but we ended the year with revenue at exactly the same level, $12,000. But the money came from different types of products compared to the first year.

Two full years into our business, it was consuming a lot of time and delivering very little money into our pockets. But it was showing signs of life. We were not under the stress of owing investors anything. It was ours to grow if we could figure out how.

In our third year, our revenue tripled as the changes we had implemented started to benefit the bottom line. We had learned new lessons that clearly helped us grow. Our little business was starting to gain real momentum.

In our fourth year, we saw revenue triple again, growing into six figures. The lessons we needed to learn got harder. Our little business transitioned from a two-person operation to a team effort. The ideas and opportunities got bigger.

As we end our fifth full year in business, we are on track to finish with another massive jump in revenue. The lessons continue to come more quickly than ever. We can envision becoming a million dollar company. We can see the problems that we'll need to solve, and we are working to address them. But the core of our work is no different than it was during the winter of 2008 when we started. At the core, we are a craft business engaging in the design and sale of unique items.

Your business journey will undoubtedly be different than ours. There is no doubt that many of you will find more success than we have and experience more rapid growth. But it won't happen without overcoming obstacles and learning hard lessons.

We would love to hear from you as your business grows. Please connect with us on social media and tell us your story.

We wish you all the best in your business endeavors,

Jason and Cinnamon Miles

P.S. If you're interested in staying connected with us and learning new lessons, as well as sharing your lessons with a community of like-minded people, then The Cutting Room might be right for you. It is where we hang out and discuss business issues with our partners and like-minded friends. You can find more information about how to sign up on www.libertyjanepartners.com

Resources by Liberty Jane Clothing

Learn more about the resources available from Liberty Jane Clothing:

The Cutting Room: The Cutting Room is a club for Liberty Jane Partners and also open to everyone interested in growing their craft business. It gives you direct access to Cinnamon and Jason as well as a whole set of additional benefits, training programs, and opportunities to learn. Learn more at http://thecuttingroom.kajabi.com/login

Liberty Jane Partners: Are you interested in joining the free Liberty Jane Partners program? Learn more about how you can make money sewing and selling doll clothes at: http://www.libertyjanepartners.com

Price It Like Picasso: Jason's first book is an in-depth explanation of our nine-step process for eBay auction success. You can buy it in Kindle format on Amazon for just $2.99. It is also available as a free resource to Cutting Room members.

Pinterest Power: In *Pinterest Power,* we chronicle our journey with Pinterest. This was our first professionally published book and it has been a top seller on Amazon since October 2012. You can buy it in several formats on Amazon.

Etsy Income Explosion: This webinar series was created to help Etsy sellers learn to fully leverage the Etsy platform to grow a substantial business. It is not a how-to use Etsy course, it is focused on how to leverage Etsy to increase overall sales and build a business that thrives beyond Etsy. This program is exclusively available to Cutting Room members.

Email Marketing Like A Pro - So Your Business Can Grow: This webinar provides an overview of how to conduct professional email marketing - with an emphasis on marketing. The program describes best practices, tip, tricks and little known, but highly valuable information. This program is exclusively available to Cutting Room members.

Start Up On Pinterest Boot Camp: This multi-part video training series provides an orientation to Pinterest from a marketing perspective and explains the basic set-up options available so marketing can occur effectively on Pinterest. This program is exclusively available to Cutting Room members.

Marketing On Pinterest Boot Camp: This multi-part video training series walks you through the marketing strategies that have helped Liberty Jane Clothing achieve massive success with Pinterest. The course walks you through the creation of a simple marketing plan that is highly effective. This program is exclusively available to Cutting Room members.

Selling On Pinterest Boot Camp: This multi-part video training series walks you through the selling related strategies available to Pinterest marketers. With step-by-step details and real examples, this course is designed to help you make sales via Pinterest. This program is exclusively available to Cutting Room members.

Marketing On Youtube: This ebook provides a marketing blueprint for effectively using Youtube to drive sales. Many crafters are finding a massive and loyal following in Youtube, and you can too. This program is exclusively available to Cutting Room members.

CPSIA information can be obtained at www.ICGtesting.com
Printed in the USA
LVOW05s0814311213

367566LV00002B/61/P

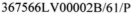